SOUTH INDIAN COINS

SOUTH INDIAN COINS

BY

DEWAN BAHADUR
SIR T. DESIKACHARI, KL., M.R.A.S.

GYAN

Published by

GYAN

Gyan Publishing House
5, Ansari Road
Daryaganj, New Delhi-110002
Phone: 011-47034999, 9811692060
E-mail: books@gyanbooks.com

Distribution Network
gyanbooks.com
India, USA, Canada, UK, Australia, France

ISBN : 978-81-212-4546-3 (HB)
First Published, 1933

2nd Impression 2020

Printed at: Gyan Press, Delhi.

The book at your disposal is the edition of an old book originally published long back. The Text quality of this book may not be at par as compared to our other books but many readers approached us to reprint this important book so that it could satiate their hunger. We request all the readers of this book to help us to improve its quality by providing the necessary text of those pages which are not properly visible. Your valuable support in this case will be highly appreciated and acknowledged and our future readers will be benefitted immensely.

SOUTH INDIAN COINS

BY

DEWAN BAHADUR

SIR T. DESIKACHARI, Kt., M.R.A.S.

TRICHINOPOLY:

St. Joseph's Industrial School Press

1933

CONTENTS

	PAGE
Proceedings of the Madras Literary Society	1
South Indian Epigraphy and Numismatics Andhras: Pallavas	7
The Chalukyas and their Coinage	38
The Cholas and their Coinage	61
The Coins of Vijaiyanagar	75
The Coins of Malabar	80
Notes on the Indo Dutch Coinage	82
Indo-French Coins	88
The Pallavas and their Coinage	113
List of Pallava Coins in the Cabinet of T. M. Rangachari and T. Desikachari	135
List of Pallava Coins in the Government Central Museum, Madras, and in the Cabinet of Dr. J. R. Henderson ...	141
Dravidian Coins by Dewan Bahadur T. M. Rangachari, B.A., and Dewan Bahadur T. Desikachari, B.A., B.L., M.R.A.S. ...	164
List of Pandiyan Coins	167
List of Chola Coins	180
Some inedited Coins of the Kings of Vijayanagara by T. M. Rangachari, B.A. and T. Desikachari, B.A., B.L. ...	186
Indo-Danish Coins by T. M. Rangachari and T. Desikachari...	192
Six plates: Illustrating Pandyan and Chola Coins in lists on pages 167—185.	

FOREWORD

THE study of South Indian numismatics is a fascinating one opening up a long succession of events to be remembered and anticipated, the vicissitudes of the history of the Peninsula of India South of the Vindhyas for over two thousand years. From the time that I read my first paper before the Madras Literary Society in 1888, I have been speaking or writing on South Indian Coins. The limited number of copies of my contributions to learned Societies or Journals has become exhausted: for year after year those who have done me the honour of visiting me and seeing my coins have been given copies of whatever I had written on the relics of a forgotten coinage illustrating South Indian history. The call came for these being collected and printed in the form of a book so that my early efforts in this still vast and unexplored field of research might be made available to students interested in South Indian coins. Among my many visitors were scholars of repute, young people qualifying for University Degrees and distinguished personages like Governors of the Province. I have therefore collected together a few of my papers read before the Madras Literary Society and articles contributed to journals of repute and issued this my first volume dealing with South Indian Numismatics to be followed at an early date by a second volume bringing the matter up-to-date and correcting or amending if needed the conclusions which I have arrived at years ago. There are many departments of Numismatic interest in my Coin Register still requiring scholarly treatment; but many preoccupations, unrelated to scholarly pursuits, did latterly so obsess me as to neglect the publication of my notes that I sometimes thought that they could be published but posthumously. Still I hope, the span of life allotted to me permitting its being done, to complete the work if at least demonstrate that there is yet a great deal to be done for our reading and understanding properly the history of the Dravida Desam from inscriptions and coins. The sole object of the present reprint of my papers, articles and notes on South Indian Coins is but to instil an enthusiasm and promote a keen desire for the reconstruction of South Indian history on the basis of such evidence as is real and not on materials as are based on mere tradition and imagination.

T. DESIKACHARI.

South Indian Coins

THE NEED FOR AN UP-TO-DATE LIST

The preparation of a connected History of the three great Dravidian Kingdoms of Southern India known as the Pandya, the Chola and the Chera is beset with considerable difficulty owing to the extreme paucity of authentic data bearing on the fortunes of these Princely houses. Puranic accounts are for various reasons of little historical utility unless confirmed by evidence obtainable from such independent sources as contemporary literature, epigraphy, or numismatics. The varied and voluminous ancient Tamil literature, while it is a valuable storehouse of information bearing on the manners and customs and religious beliefs of the ancients is not free from the characteristic shortcomings of Indian writings where chronology and history are concerned. Epigraphy has so far not served very much towards the elucidation of early Dravidian History the oldest inscription not carrying us very much further back than the 10th century A.D.

In this state of almost total dearth of reliable historical material one would have hoped that the numismatic record of the Peninsula would be of help in verifying at least the reality of the personages treated of in the Puranas, having regard particularly to the large variety and great number of examples of the South Indian monetary system still extant. Though it may be asserted with tolerable certainty that some at least of the Madura and Tinnevelly coins, the rectangular copper and the silver punch marked money, were current at the time when Buddhism and Jainism were the prevailing faiths of the land, yet the absence of all legend on these coins baffles any attempt at fixing their age or the names of those who had issued them. All that they teach us is that at the period of their circulation the decadence in art which, in South India, was probably synchronous with the persecution and the gradual extinction of the Jainas had not commenced. The well-out-lined and freely drawn figures of the elephant and the bull and other devices peculiar to Buddhism bear comparison with similar symbols on the lead coinage of the Andhra dynasty which was predominant in the central table land till the 3rd century A.D. So great is the similarity that one is tempted to ascribe to both a common origin.

Having in view the high artistic merit of this copper money there can be no doubt that a ruder coinage had preceded it and there was probably an interval between the age when seminal and testaceous exponents of value were actually used in the daily transactions of the community and the time when a finished metallic currency was in vogue. But of this earlier, if ruder, coinage all trace has been lost.

Of the money ascribable to a later age we have a great variety with and without legend. The legends in the Pandiyan coins appear to be no more than titular designations by which a monarch was known or desired to be known for some exploit real or fancied. Instances are not wanting in which coins bearing the same legend have by different numismatic peculiarities to be attributed to by reigns and even ages. Add to this another disconcerting element in the investigation, the absence of any date on these coins and the magnitude is realised of the obstacle in the way of determining the age of the coin, and appreciating the true import of the legend or device on it.

Of genuine coins of the old Chera Kingdom none have come to light, while the Chola money discovered up-to-date belong to the period of Chola ascendancy in the South between the 9th and 11th centuries.

It will be our aim, in these pages, to present together all the available information in respect of the coinage of the three great Dravidian Kingdoms of Southern India, as well as to hold a brief survey of the coinage of the numerous petty sovereignties which after the subversion of the paramount powers, began to issue each its own money, inundating the Tamil country thus with a variety of coins whose due tabulation is, to the numismatic enquirer, at first sight, not a little perplexing. We shall make the list of examples which have hitherto come to light fairly exhaustive if only to make it serve as a landmark where from future numismatists might start their investigation into the monetary system of the Tamils.

The first systematic and comprehensive treatment of South Indian coins was due to the late Sir Walter Elliot who embodied the results of his life long, intelligent and laborious research in his contribution to the Numismata Orientalia, nearly twenty years ago. Since then our knowledge of the subject has been augmented both by accession to the list of the coins of the Dravidian Kingdoms and by more accurate readings of those published by him. This addition to our stock of information lies however scattered in contributions to different journals and in the coin catalogues of a few coin collectors who have strenuously endeavoured to rescue from the brasier's pot and the goldsmith's crucible a small proportion of these relics of an extinct civilization and forgotten Empires. It will be thus apparent that while the work of Sir Walter Elliot must always hold its place as the text book on South Indian Numismatics it is essential to have our knowledge of the subject brought up-to-date and presented in a compendious and easily accessible form to those interested in archæological studies.

A work with the above avowed object were still incomplete did it not include a brief resume of the results of epigraphical research and the study of ancient Tamil literature so far as they might bear on the history of the Dravidian Powers of whose coinage we treated. However disappointing the information available from these sources compared with the number of inscriptions copied and published and the voluminous body of ancient indigenous literature we have still a nucleus to start with, which let us hope, further research may at some future time help to develop and enlarge.

* PROCEEDINGS OF THE MADRAS LITERARY SOCIETY, 7th JANUARY, 1916.

SOUTH INDIAN HISTORY.

EPIGRAPHY AND NUMISMATICS.

Diwan Bahadur T. Desikachari, of Trichinopoly, an ardent student of numismatics, delivered an interesting address yesterday at the Senate House, under the auspices of the Madras Literary Society, on "South Indian Epigraphy and Numismatics." His Excellency the Governor presided, and among those who attended were Her Excellency Lady Pentland, Mr. and Mrs. Lionel Vibert, Captain W. S. E. Money, Mr. T. E. Moir, Sir V. C. Desikachariar, the Hon'ble Justice Kumaraswami Sastri, Mrs. Annie Besant, Dewan Bahadur T. M. Rangachari, Mr. Hadaway, Dr. Henderson, Professor Krishnaswami Ayangar, Mr. Gopinada Rao, Mr. C. P. Ramaswami Aiyar, Professor Ramanadan, Professor Hanumanta Rao, Rao Bahadur Bhavanandam Pillai, Rao Bahadur Muniswami Aiyar, and Rao Saheb Ramanujam Chetti.

THE DISCUSSION.

His Excellency the Governor then invited the gentlemen present to offer any remarks they might have on the lecture.

Mr. Lionel Vibert, himself an old numismatist, said that there were really no satisfactory catalogues to help them in the pioneer work that was being

* Adapted from the Madras Mail of the 8th January 1916.

conducted into the study of South Indian coinage of ancient times. In the absence of catalogues they have to turn to workers like Diwan Bahadur T. Desikachari. Until a catalogue was produced, they had only to collect and theorise. They had very often no names of the Kings or of the mints on several of the coins. Mr. Vibert recommended the study of coins as a delightful hobby. He hoped that a Numismatical Society would be started in Southern India, similar to that which flourished in Northern India and the one in Ceylon. Ceylon had been so intimately connected with South India in the early times that it was not possible to study the numismatics of the latter thoroughly without also studying the early Ceylon coins; and die-struck pieces in Ceylon were also found along with the small Roman coins to which allusion had been made in the paper. Coins often throw remarkable light by way of supplementing historical inscriptions, as the history of St. Thomas, which mentioned the name of a South Indian King unknown to students received remarkable verification from a discovery of a coin on which Sir Walter Elliot found the name of the King inscribed. There was need for more workers in the field, and he hoped that several would take to it.

Mr. J. R. Henderson speaking of the Roman coins, expressed strong doubts of the theory that the Romans had actually struck coins in India. He believed that the Pandiyan Kings were not likely to have allowed the Romans to strike coins at their capital when the Pandiyans themselves had their own currency. Indian Kings had always been very zealous of the prerogative of coinage. Those who maintained the theory that the Romans had struck coins in Madura should come forward with a coin on which something could be seen and deciphered, and submit the same to a European expert.

Sir V. C. Desikachariar pointed out that the study of numismatics, apart from its historical had a practical value also. He said that he had been able to establish the impartibility of the Ramnad Zamindari by a study of ancient coins, from which he collected evidence as to the Ramnad Zamindars' right to coinage in earlier times. A study of numismatics showed how contented had been the people of India and how ancient India had been a land of plenty. Chakrams, Amman Kasu, Koil Kasu, etc., were the lowest coins. In Pudukottah, in decades gone by, Amman Kasu used to be distributed with the doles of rice. An Amman Kasu had been thought to give sufficient to buy all the necessaries for a meal for which a dole of rice was made. The purchasing power of an Amman Kasu must have been sufficiently high to enable a man to get a hearty meal with its aid. Now-a-days with a few Chakrams and Amman Kasus given with a dole of rice, no man could get even a half meal. He referred to the Indian King called Nanda, who had used leather pieces to strike coins with.

The lecturer, in reply, observed that he was grateful to Dr. Henderson for his learned criticism, that some of the grounds in support of the theory that Colonies of Roman merchants and soldiers must have settled in and around the principal marts in South India and Ceylon were briefly set forth in the lecture, that in such matters none could predicate with certainty or dogmatise with authority and that the demolition of a pet theory on rational grounds was as great an asset in scientific investigation as the formulation of a tentative one, but that further research, judging from existing evidence, is likely to establish the correctness of the views advocated by the lecturer.

THE GOVERNOR.

His Excellency Lord Pentland, in his concluding remarks, pointed out that the lecturer of the evening and Mr. Vibert had by their remarks done much to strip the study of numismatics of those terrors with which, largely owing to its scientific terminology, it was usually associated. Sir V. C. Desikachariar had shown as an additional inducement that a knowledge of numismatics could be turned to practical use. The cordiality with which the lecture had been received would, His Excellency hoped, reward the lecturer for the labour he had bestowed upon it. A great deal had been done during the last fifty years by workers such as Diwan Bahadur T. Desikachariar in the field of numismatics and by others, both officials and non-officials, in other fields to render available the raw materials of the history of the civilisation of South India; but a great deal still remained to be done. The Epigraphical Department of the Government of Madras, for example, had collected stores of raw materials which, at present, to a great extent, lay unutilised. They had many inscriptions to translate and to make known to the growing circle of workers in historical research from whose ranks we might hope that in days to come some one would come forward competent to undertake that comprehensive history of South India, which was so greatly to be desired. For the materials of that work, reliance would have to be placed to a large extent on inscriptions, architecture and coins. The increasing interest taken by Indian gentlemen in these studies was therefore a most gratifying feature. After all, the position with reference to the history of India was very much the same as it had been in respect of the history of Greek civilisation about fifty years ago. Those who were acquainted with the subject knew how much had been done in these fifty years by exploration and excavation and other means to elucidate and to fill up gaps which existed in the picture presented of the Homeric civilisation. In the same way and by similar means, they were now filling up the great gaps which existed in Indian History, and he would ask them to join in according a vote of thanks to Diwan Bahadur T. Desikachariar for his contribution to that work. If it led to a fuller recognition of what had been done and still remained to be done, he felt sure that the lecturer would be amply rewarded for his labours. His Excellency was convinced that a fuller and more accurate knowledge of the past history of this country would help them to meet in a spirit of greater sympathy and understanding the problems which had to be dealt with in the future.

SOUTH INDIAN EPIGRAPHY AND NUMISMATICS.

DIWAN BAHADUR T. DESIKA CHARI.

My purpose this evening is to take a general survey of what has been achieved by epigraphical and numismatical studies in Southern India during the past twenty-five years. They alone can furnish true and unerring evidence bearing on the history and civilisation of the Dravida country during the past two thousand years; of sovereignties which, while leaving their indelible marks on the life of the people and their hopes and aspirations in the Peninsula of India, are remembered but in name, from what time the ideals of Priyadasin were promulgated by his edicts till when Christian Missionaries like Schwartz and Dubois laboured in Southern India, from the time of the Andhras to the fall of the last great Hindu kingdom of Vijayanagara through the period of the incessant and demoralising contest for power between the numerous petty chieftains each of whom strove to be independent or supreme, till the advent of the rival trading East India Companies and during all the vicissitudes of the war of the Carnatic ending in the final establishment of the British Indian Empire.

I propose this evening to deal with the period from the earliest times of which any record has survived to us till the 8th century A. D.

Twenty-seven years ago I had the privilege of reading before this Society a paper on 'Indo-Danish Coins' under the joint names of myself and Diwan Bahadur T. M. Rangachariar, whom, I am happy to address in 1916, as one of the members of the Society. I feel proud to appear under the auspices of the same Society more than a quarter of a century after my maiden effort in South Indian numismatics and under the presidency of Your Excellency.

Graduates of Indian Universities devoting their spare time and energy—very little of the same could be spared from their bread-winning pursuits to the study of epigraphy and numismatics—enjoy the rare advantage of the possession of instinctive and patriotic veneration for the relics of their past history and familiarity with its religious beliefs and social traditions and usages so essentially required for catching the spirit of ancient inscriptions and coins and studying them with an insight into their real meaning with sympathy and understanding. During the last quarter of a century the number of graduates taking interest in these departments of original research has shown a marked increase, but it is still small. Thousands of inscriptions and coins have been collected through official agency and by private collectors. They have to be examined systematically and studied comprehensively, a work which has not been attempted so far.

A quarter of a century ago the information available about the history of South Indian dynasties was very meagre. A reference to Mr. Sewell's sketch of South Indian dynasties officially compiled and a perusal of the District Manuals of that time will bear out this assertion. The Gazetteers which have replaced these District Manuals have assimilated the materials furnished by inscriptions in the very limited way in which alone it could be done. The considered conclusions of a quarter of a century ago have had to be abandoned or modified in the light of facts gleaned from inscriptions.

A quarter of a century ago, Sir Walter Elliot's contribution on South Indian coins to the Numismata Orientalia represented the sum of our knowledge on the subject. Since then important additions have been made to our materials for research in this department of study. The collection in the Government Central Museum has been augmented in the number and quality of its specimens. The cabinets of private collectors like Mr. T. M. Rangachariar and Mr. Lionel Vibert, I. C. S., have grown.

An up-to-date catalogue of the coins in these collections will be of great use to students interested in original research. Mr. Thurston attempted, years ago, to do this for the coins of the Government Central Museum. Nearly twelve years ago, he and I prepared lists of the Pandyan, Chola, Pallava and Vijayanagara coins and those of the Setupatis and Madura Nayaks. He had intended to take them up after publishing the coins of the various East India Companies and those of Mysore. It is hoped Dr. Henderson who is himself a keen Numismatist could publish these lists in due time.

I have tried to prepare and publish catalogues of the Pandya, Chola and Pallava coins, but by the very nature of the limitations that an amateur labours under, I could not make them as full as I should desire to make them.

Isolated departments of study have received special and scholarly treatment at the hands of Dr. Fleet, Dr. Hultzsch, the late Rao Bahadur Venkayya and of Rao Saheb Krishna Sastri and Mr. S. Krishnaswami Aiyangar. But what remains to be achieved is the construction of a connected and continuous history of the various ancient sovereignties illumined by the volume and wealth of material collected in British India and the States of Mysore, Travancore and Puducotta.

Let us take an imaginary map of South India at the time of the Andhra ascendency. The Andhra kings were contemporaries of the Dravidian kings of the Chola, Chera and Pandyan lines. Into the country in which these wielded sway, came the Pallavas and the Chalukyas; later on rose the Vijayanagara Empire: side by side with the rise and growth of Muhammadan influence in the south, with the usurpation of power both by the Delhi and Vijayanagar Viceroys.

The fall of Vijayanagara and disruption among its enemies, were followed by a state of confusion and anarchy which favoured the trading companies of the west in their attempt to acquire territory and rule over them. The various Poligars of the South and petty chieftains of the north and the Mysore usurpers Hyder and Tippu have to be allotted their own places in the shifting and kaleidoscopic panorama of history during the past two thousand years.

Inscriptions or coins or both have been found illustrating many of the main events in the conflict which was going on all along for domination and power. Have in view the momentous political and social changes which must have been going on in the meanwhile. The marvel is not that many thousands of inscriptions and coins have already been collected, but that some periods of history are unrepresented; while with regard to others the number which has survived is so small.

The earliest lithic records in South India are the edicts of Asoka issued by the great Buddhist Emperor in order to promulgate his message of peace, love, charity and truth, to all his neighbouring realms among whom he enumerated the Pandyas, the Cholas and Keralas as independent kings. These edicts are in the *prakrit*, the spoken Sanskrit, as opposed to its classical form.

These records, which in South India are found in the modern Ganjam District and the present Mysore Province, refer to the three great Dravidian Kingdoms of the South and show the extent to which Buddhistic influences permeated into the southern portion of the Peninsula and probably shaped its religion, politics and society for all time.

The natural caves with artificial stone beds, familiarly known as the '*Pancha Pandava beds*' or the beds of the five Pandava heroes of the national epic, Mahabharata, in inaccessible rocks in many of the Southern Districts are of peculiar interest to the students alike of South Indian epigraphy and architecture. These so-called beds are in some instances too narrow and too short to serve as such, and more than five of them are found carved in some of the caves. Their association with the Pandava brothers is probably due more to the number of beds found in the majority of the caves than any tradition that they had really occupied them. They were probably the resting places of ascetics or mendicants who took to a life of meditation and solitude.

Some of these beds bear Brahmi inscriptions, the alphabet resembling that of the Asoka edicts. These are probably the earliest extant lithic records in the Tamil country. Similar caves of decidedly Buddhist origin with Pali inscriptions in the Brahmi character have been discovered in Ceylon. A wave of Buddhism seems to have swept over the Southern Peninsula on to the island of Ceylon from the time of Asoka; and its influence was sufficiently potent and lasting to enable Buddhist priests or mendicants to settle in the heart of the Tamil country.

The characters inscribed are fairly legible, but the purport thereof is unintelligible up to now as observed by Mr. Krishna Sastri in his latest report on Southern Indian epigraphy. That Pali was understood in South India in the palmy days of Buddhism is itself a noteworthy fact. What influence the script used in these Brahmi records exerted on the indigenous 'Vattalettu' Tamil alphabet of the Pandyan country is a problem intimately connected with the origin of the Dravidians themselves. Whether the 'Vattalettu' or the early Tamil alphabet was introduced into the Tamil country from Northwestern Semitic sources or was derived from the Asoka or Brahmi characters above referred to is an investigation of exceeding interest. The Pallava Tamil and the later Grandha Tamil were both affected by the North Indian alphabet and indeed they may be termed offshoots thereof; but the 'Vattalettu' has ceased to exist and is only preserved in lithic records of a period anterior to the tenth century A. D. Suffice it, for the present purpose, to state that the "Brahmi" was probably used for some centuries before and after the Christian Era by Buddhist missionaries and Brahmins subsequent to the date of the Asoka edicts, and that the 'Vattalettu' alone introduced centuries before Asoka from Western Asia into Southern India, uninfluenced by other scripts, was the indigenous alphabet of the Tamils and was probably the one in use side by side with the characters adopted in the edicts of Asoka and the "Pancha Pandava beds" above referred to. In this connection the appearance of inscriptions in Vattalettu at or near these Pancha Pandava beds referring to Jaina teachers is of great significance.

If the Brahmi records do not throw much light on the history of the times ascribable to them, we at least learn from them that Buddhistic influences were at work in the Tamil country. They suggest immense possibilities. The message of Asoka was appreciated by the Dravidians who had already advanced in civilization. The result was that Dravida had the benefit of her own advanced civilization as well as that of all that the north could teach it.

The coins attributable to the same period do not advance our knowledge any further. Many centuries before the art of coining was appreciated as an indispensable requisite of commercial intercourse, measures of value in the precious metals must have commended themselves to every civilization as media of exchange alike unfluctuating in value and compact in form. When this stage was reached in the Dravida country and whether the references in the Code of Manu and in ancient Buddhist literature to *Swarnas* and Kahapanas or Karshapanas were but to measures of value and not actual current coins are fields of enquiry which open up as wide a vista of possibilities, even as do the problems relating to the origin of the Dravidians, the introduction of writing into their land and the effect of the Brahmi or the North Indian alphabet on 'Vattalettu.'

The oldest coins found in the Southern Districts so far, are flat, thin, rectangular, quadrilateral or irregularly shaped silver pieces weighing between 50 to 60 grains bearing distinctively Buddhistic devices incused or 'punched' on them. The stamps or punches are placed separately or are superimposed one over the other. Such marks denoted the agency through which the coins passed into circulation, or the successive guilds, reigns, or territories through which they continued to be current. The 'punches' do not seem to have been placed all simultaneously. They were apparently imprinted on them at different times to indicate the chequered career of each piece.

The coins are worn so thin and smooth that if any date or legend there were on these coins, they are no longer decipherable on them.

I have elsewhere attempted to show that the indigenous Dravidian standards of measures of weight and value, based on seminal and testaceous exponents of value (such as the mustard, barley-corn and the bean or cowries of sorts) were not a little influenced by the metrical and monetary standards, of the Phœnicians, with whom the Dravidians had from the earliest times an intimate trading relationship across the Arabian sea.

On the specimens in a fair state of preservation are noticeable the Chakra, Chaitya, Swastika, the Bo-tree, the elephant, the horse and other emblems familiar to Buddhist hiorogrammy and assigned a prominent place in Buddhist sculpture. The serpent and the *trisul* are also the emblems which are seen imprinted on these specimens. These thin silver pieces occur throughout India from the frontiers of Baluchistan to Cape Comorin. "They have been discovered among the ashes of the men who constructed the primitive tombs known as 'kulies' or (kistavens) of the south and unearthed from the ruins of buried cities in excavating the head-waters of Ganges canal."

All that we learn from the symbols and devices on these coins and their occurrence over such a wide area is that at one time a uniform standard prevailed and that at that time Buddhism had exercised a considerable influence throughout India, a standard which has influenced the 'fish,' 'boar' and 'tiger' coins of later times. They were probably synchronous with the Pancha Pandava beds and Brahmi inscriptions adverted to above.

Equally remarkable as the silver coins dealt with above, are a series die-struck and rectangular in shape, which turn up from time to time in the Southern Districts and Ceylon.

These coins again do not bear dates. They occur in three sizes, the largest weighing 180 grains.

"In the Punjab rectangular coins weighing about 180 grains are often found. They have on one side an elephant in high relief, on the other a lion incuse. Both animals have a Buddhist symbol over them. Sometimes a horse takes the place of the lion and above it is a star. Other rectangular coins have still other devices on one side only, the other side being plain."

On the specimens discovered in South India appear on the obverse well-executed figures of the elephant with or without riders and attendants, the bull, the horse and the sacred tree together with, on the field and in the exergue, symbols of the Buddhistic faith.

On some specimens appear legends in characters similar to those used in the Brahmi inscriptions already referred to, but they are not decipherable without the help of better specimens for comparison and scrutiny.

The mounted figures and the artistic finish and perfect form of the devices on all these coins lead to the conclusion that they belonged to a period in which still Buddhism and its influence were strongly felt and when with the impetus given by contact with the Yavanas, there arose a school of art noted alike for the accuracy of its design and the chastity of its subject.

Compared with the extent of Asoka's Empire, the territories governed by the Dravidian Kings of the south, sink into the level of principalities of very modest dimensions. But the Great "Priyadasin" recognized them as independent sovereignties and neighbouring realms as early as the third century B. C. Among the monasteries he founded, was one in the Tanjore District consecrated by his brother Mahendra. From ancient Tamil Literature and contemporary evidence it is tolerably certain that these Dravidian Kings continued in a flourishing condition for some centuries after the commencement of the Christian era, till they came into conflict with the Pallavas and the Chalukyas. Still no epigraphical or numismatic evidence has so far been forthcoming from these times till we reach the ninth century.

But the same period witnessed the growth and fall of three powerful dynasties, *viz.*, the Andhras, the Chalukyas and the Pallavas: the decay of Buddhism and extinction of Jainism and the revival of the Brahminical Faith in the forms in which it has come down to us in the present day.

Before however dealing with the coinage of the Andhras and the Pallavas, reference has to be made to the small copper coins of insignificant value still unearthed in and around Madura which by their type and the characters of the legends on them—unfortunately too far gone to be decipherable—must be assigned a Roman origin. Though there have been finds of *aureii* and *denarii* in many Districts of South India, in Madura and Ceylon and the Coromandel Coast alone are these small copper pieces to be met with. It is noteworthy too that among the authentic finds of Roman coins in South India nowhere have copper coins of the regular coinage been found side by side with these small copper pieces as in Madura.

In our own collection we have aureii of Zeno, Anastasius and Theodosius all acquired in Madura; a copper coin of the regular Imperial coinage with, on the obverse, the head of a female figure and the legend *Europa Roma* and, on the reverse, the figure of a she wolf suckling *Romulus* and *Remus*, found in Devipatam; and a number of small pieces with the figure of the Emperor's head on the obverse and two standing figures spear in hand on the reverse; others too with a single standing figure or the diagram similar to what appears on the die-struck square copper coins adverted to above, are among the coins so far discovered.

Mr. R. Sewell, I.C.S. (Retired) has collected all the information available on the Roman coins found in India and has appended to his contribution on the subject to the journal of the Royal Asiatic Society a list of such coins. A cursory glance at this list will show that in the Southern Districts and particularly in the Pandya and Chera country it was that most of the coins were unearthed. He has, however, not seen any of the small copper under reference, which Captain Tufnell and I had seen and discussed.

That there was a considerable trade between the Dravidian Kingdoms of the South and Rome in the early centuries of the Christian era, in pepper, spices, fine muslins, perfumes, unguents, pearls and precious stones especially the beryl, admits of little doubt. Almost all these articles were products of South India. The Pandyans were perhaps predominant amongst the "Muvvarasars" or the three Kings of the South. "The most highly prized of the stones was the beryl only found in India in Padinadu or Padiyur in the Coimbatore District and these beryls were believed to be the best in the world. A large number of *aureii* and *denarii* have been found in the neighbourhood of these mines." The author of the Periplus in A. D. 80, speaks of Muziris, the nearest port to Madura on the West Coast as a city at the height of prosperity, while the Pandyan and Chera Kings were spoken of by Pliny, the latter by name, Madura being mentioned as the Pandyan Capital. Ptolemy who states that he obtained his knowledge from persons who had "resided" in India a long time (from those that sailed thither and frequented their places for a long time and from those who came from thence to us) gives the names of places in the neighbourhood of Madura and the interior of South India."

To such an extent were the wealth and importance born of foreign commercial intercourse developed in Southern India that in the early centuries of the Christian era Yavana (Roman or Greek) mercenaries were tempted to serve under the Pandyan fish banner and mount guard on the lofty towers of Madura. A highly developed monarchical Government aided by popular assemblies is assumed in ancient Tamil Literature as the heritage of ages. The acts of peace no less than of war seem to have been assiduously cultivated and glowing descriptions occur in early temple literature of richly-laden merchantmen visiting the Emporia of the East and West Coasts of the Dravida country. So great and lasting was the Roman influence in South India, that even after the ninth century A. D. inscriptions record the gift of *dinaras* and *drammas* for religious and charitable benefactions.

Having regard to all the above considerations, I ventured to think along with Captain Tufnell that a colony of Roman merchants and soldiers must have settled in Madura in the palmy days of the Pandyan rule. Finding this expression of opinion in a brochure of mine on the Pandya and Chola coins, Dr. Henderson wrote to me as follows:—

"I find on page 18 reference to what has always seemed to be of the most interesting of the still unsolved problems in South Indian numismatics *viz.*, lack of knowledge of the Pandyan coins which were issued between the commencement of the Christian Era and the 12th century A. D. The square Madura coins which appear to have been copied from the Taxila series must belong to the former period if they are not earlier and then follows a great gap in our knowledge lasting for many centuries. The Pandyans must have struck coins during this interval as some of their contemporaries did. But where are they? In spite of what numerous writers have said, I am inclined to doubt if the Romans actually struck coins in India. I believe the theory rests chiefly on the incorrect assumption that the small copper coins found in Madura and Ceylon belong to a type unknown in Europe. Moreover they belong, I believe, to the Byzantine period when Roman trade with India had considerably declined."

There is however nothing startling in the theory advanced by me. If there was a considerable commercial intercourse between Madura and Rome in the early centuries of the Christian era, if Yavana soldiers could be got to mount guard on the gates of the

Madura Fort and if encouragement were offered to Roman trade by the conditions of South India by the Pallavas and the Andhras as well as by the Muvvarasars, there was every probability of Roman merchants and soldiers forming themselves into a colony in Madura and other marts of that time under sovereign protection as western traders did in later times when settlements arose in Madras, Fort St. David, Tranquebar, Negapatam and Goa. For mercantile transactions with traders receiving the Roman coinage the regular copper money would have served efficiently. For the transactions of the small settlements of traders in the principal cities or marts such as household purchases and the exigencies of ordinary life which necessitate the use of small change, a separate currency was perhaps necessary. No doubt Roman gold and silver coins so naturalised themselves in South India as to be used centuries later as pointed above. But this does not militate against the assumption that small copper of such trifling value as that of thin worn-out pieces under reference conld not have been imported for use in mercantile transactions.

There was every facility, moreover, for minting coins in Madura. The square Buddhist die-struck coins of the same period were probably struck in the Pandyan country.

Trade no doubt was on the wane in the Byzantine period. But there was still enough left apparently in pepper and spices to attract the gold coins of the period to the Madura country. As yet it is not possible to assert definitely that these small pieces belonged to that period and not to that antecedent to that of the Emperor Nero. These are some of the considerations which made me think that the coins in question were probably intended for use in a colony or settlement of local merchants and soldiers.

Even if these coins were not struck locally they might have been minted in Europe for use in the Roman Settlements in the East. At a later period such a thing actually happened. The Dutch East India Company when they required money for circulation in their East India Settlements seem to have minted the numerous series of thin copper money known as "Dutch challies" and imported the same into India.

In a matter of this kind it is not possible to make a more definite statement and we must leave the subject here in the hope, that further research will throw more light in the matter.

I shall now pass on to the Andhras.

THE ANDHRAS.

Professor Rapson in his recent book on "Ancient India" has the following account of the Andhras:— "The decline of the Maurya Empire was marked also by the rapid growth of the Andhra kingdom in South India. Originally a Dravidian people living immediately to the south of the Kalingas in that part of the Madras Presidency which lies between the rivers Godavari and Krishna the Andhras became, probably about 200 B. C., a great power whose territories included the whole of the Deccan and extended to the Western Coast. They are mentioned in the edicts of Asoka in a manner which seems to indicate that they acknowledged the suzerainty of Asoka, but that they were never conquered and brought under the direct Government of a Viceroy of the Empire of Asoka as their neighbours, the Kalingas. They would seem to have asserted their independence soon after the death of Asoka. Some outline of their history may be traced by the aid of their inscriptions, coins and literary sources from probably 220 B. C. to 220 A. D. The names of a succession of thirty kings are preserved in the Puranas, together with the length of each reign and the total duration of the dynasty is given as 456 or 460 years. The Puranas are usually in agreement with the evidence of inscriptions and coins, so far as the names of the kings and the length of their reigns are concerned, but they assign to the dynasty a chronological position which is impossible."

This fairly sums up the knowledge in brief which we have about the Andhras from unerring sources of history in the words of one who has carefully studied the inscriptions and coins of the Andhras and prepared a list of them published in the British Museum Catalogue in 1908.

These Andhra kings were generally known as the Sātavahanas or Sātakarnis. Near Amaravati in the modern Guntur District, was Dhānyakataka (Dharanikota) one of their capitals; the other capitals were probably, Pratishthāna, the modern Paithan on the Godavari in the Aurangabad District of the Nizam's Dominions and Vaijayanti, the modern Banavasi in the North Canara District of the Bombay Presidency. These two were respectively the capitals of their Western and South-western Empire.

The Hathigumpha inscription of Kharavela King of Kalinga, dated about B. C. 168 shows that the third king of the Andhras was a comtemporary of the third king of the Kalingas and Sātakarni is therein termed the protector of the West. This date is the chief point in the chronological history of the Andhras. The Nanaghat inscription refers to the Queen Naganika, the wife of King Sātakarni, son of King Simukha Sātavahana and the mother of two princes Saktisri and Vedasri. The Nasik inscription gives the name of the King Kanha (Krsna) of the Sātavahana race attributed by Buhler on epigraphical grounds to the times of the last Mauryas as the earliest Sungas in the beginning of the second century B. C. The first three names are referred to in the Puranas, Srimukha, Krshna and Sri Sātakarni.

Between the earlier and later group of inscriptions of the Andhra dynasty there comes a long interval during which also no coins have been found which could be dated with precision. The Puranas alone have to be looked to for information regarding this period of history.

The later inscriptions are dated in the regnal years of the kings. The determination of their chronology depends chiefly on the inscriptions of their contemporaries and rivals the Western Satraps and from Gotamiputra's conquest of one of them, Nahapana, in the 18th year of the reign of the former who, ascended the throne probably in A. D. 106. The extent of his dominions indicated by his titles mentioned in the inscription of his mother 'Balasri' in which he is styled the king of many places named, which include the present provinces of Guzerat, portions of Malwa in Central India, Berar, the Northern Konkan and the portion of the Bombay Presidency lying south of Nasik, dominions which had been governed by Nahapana before his defeat. From the names of the mountains mentioned, he was truly the Dakshinā pathapati—the lord of the Deccan—the hereditary title of the Sātvahanas. There can be no doubt that the Andhra power was at its highest during his reign and his latest date is probably 130 A. D. The numismatic evidence for this period is meagre and imperfect, but is still interesting as directly showing in the re-struck coins the transference of the rule over Western India from Nahapana to Gotamiputra. His exploits are described as of one who crushed down the pride and concert of the Kshatrias, who destroyed the Sakas, Yavanas and Pahlavas (Scythian, Greek and Persian invaders), who rooted the Khakhavātā (Nahapana) family and who restored the glory of the Sātavahana race by the reconquest of the Andhra dominions which had been seized by the Ksaharatas.

Vāsishtiputra Sri Pulumavi was the son of Gotamiputra and ruled twenty-four years from A.D. 131. He seems to have been twice defeated by his father-in-law Rudradaman and lost some of the dominions acquired by his father. The Pudumayi of Paitan (Pratishtana) referred to by Ptolemy was probably this king.

Coins (but no inscriptions) indicate the rulers of Siva Sri Satakarni and Sri Candra Sati probably brothers of Pulumavi, as they are also styled Vāsishtiputra.

Historical memorials are more abundant for Gotamiputra Sri Yagna Satakarni. The inscriptions don't give any dates, but we learn from the Puranas that he ruled for twenty-seven years. His coins have been found in Andhra Desam, and his inscriptions in the Kistna District and Nasik and Kanheri.

Till the end of the second century A.D., the Sātavahana dynasty seems to have been the supreme power uninterruptedly from the beginning. There was a division of the Empire after Yagna Sri. The latest coins of the Andhras are of Sri Rudra Sātakarni, Sri Krsna Sātakarni and Sri Candra Sātakarni all found in Andhra Desam, the country of the Andhras.

Inscriptions in the western and southern districts of the Empire testify to the existence of another family of Sātakarnis of the Cutu race of which three generations including two reigns are known to have existed. The connection between these two Sātavahana families is uncertain. Probably the later family was a feudatory of the former family and gained independence on the death of Yagna Sri.

The large lead coins of the Anantapur and Cuddapah Districts have a doubtful reading 'Hariti.' Perhaps they refer to Haritiputra Siva Skanda Varman and Haritiputra Vishnu Kaḍ-Cuṭukula Sātakarni.

In the Madras Presidency the coins found are generally in lead; those found in the Central Provinces are in lead and an alloy called 'poten.'

The lead coins generally bear on their obverse the figures of the horse and lion, the bow-string with the arrow, the Chaitya and the Bo-tree. The ship and the Swastika are found chiefly on coins found in the

Coromandel Coast. This region was in the hands of the Cholas in the third century B.C. Before the middle of the second century it probably passed into the hands of the Pallavas; and the Andhras during the time of Pulumavi seem to have temporarily extended their power to Cholamandalam. As I shall presently show, coins with a two-masted ship are found in Mahabalipuram and are attributable to the Pallavas. The feudatories of the Andhras are perhaps responsible for the coins with the "bull" obverse.

Thus the coinage of the Andhras falls itself into distinct groups showing different epochs and they are the earliest coins of South India bearing legends giving dynastic names coupled with religious devices.

They, like the rest of the coinage of the period, bear Buddhist emblems. The prevailing metal used for the Andhra currency was lead, though issues in gold, silver and "poten" are referred to in the published lists. The specimens I have come across are all in lead, some of the "bow and arrow" or Vilvayakura type and others bearing well executed figures of the lamp (representing justice), the horse, the bull or a two-masted ship accompanied by Buddhistic devices The silver issues of Yagna Sri imitating the Satrap coinage form a distinct type indicating the conquest of the Western Satraps by Gotamiputra, a fact which is illustrated also by the re-struck coins already referred to. It is noteworthy that some of the names in the list of Andhra princes are represented by coins alone and not by inscriptions and the personal names of others have to be ascertained from the legends on their coins, the inscriptions mentioning only the family names by their mothers, a practice determined by probably some rule of succession similar to that of the Marumakkatayam law prevailing in the West Coast, judging from the names already referred to, *viz.*, Gotamiputra-Vāsishtiputra and Mādhaviputra. Professor Rapson's lists from which mainly I have prepared the above summary present at one glance all that has been done for the history of thc Andhras by epigraphy and numismatics and what remains still to be done.

That a metal so easily liable to decay as lead was used as a medium of currency by a race of so powerful and prosperous is a subject which cannot be omitted without a few remarks.

The author of the Periplus mentions tin and lead among the imports of Baragaza (Baroch) on the West Coast, and of Nelkunda (conjectured by Col. Yule to have been between Kaneth and Kolum in Travancore). Sir Walter Elliot refers to a passage in Pliny to the effect that India had neither brass nor lead, receiving them in exchange for precious stones and pearls. Coming to later times, we meet with a lead currency with the advent of the various European powers in the East. The Indo-Portuguese and Indo-Danish Companies are known to have issued lead money and the English East India Company in imitation of the Portuguese obtained of Charles II a charter anthorising them to coin among others, budgrooks "(Port Bazarucco)," lead coins, which appear to have been issued by the English East India Company in the reign of Charles II and in those of the first three Georges for currency in the Settlement of Bombay. Whether the scarcity of lead felt in the early centuries of the

Christian era, continued up to so late a period as the sixteenth and seventeenth centuries is not known, but it is not improbable that lead was still a popular medium of currency and it was to suit their customers that the earliest European power in India struck lead coins.

I shall now pass on to the Pallavas.

THE PALLAVAS.

In the eventful period of South Indian history between the second and tenth centuries of the Christian era, the Pallavas played no insignificant part in building an Empire in that portion of the Madras Presidency which lies between the Godavari on the North, the Pandyan boundary on the South with their three capitals, Conjeevaram in the Chingleput District, Vengi in the Godavari District and Palghat in Malabar. It is remarkable that a race, brave and adventurous, who enjoyed without doubt a high degree of civilisation have become so merged in the population that they are now remembered only by their coins and inscriptions, copper-plates and monolithic temples.

The monolithic structures ascribable to the times of Narasimhavarman II and known as the Seven Pagodas excite the admiration of the student of art; the caves on the Trichinopoly Rock are fine specimens of the architecture of the times of Mahendravarman "Guna Bhara;" the cave temple of Kunnandar Koil in the Pudukotah State has a graceful representation of an evidently royal personage standing in a suppliant attitude; the inscription in the Trichinopoly cave temple in Pallavagrandha characters records in verse that the King had a statue of himself and a statue of Iswara installed in the niches in the cave Mandapam, both of which, however, are no longer there; in a similar cave temple in Sevalipaiti in the Ramnad District, besides the image of Vishnu in one of the niches, it is reported that there is a dancing figure of Siva though the image in the shrine itself has as in the case of the Trichinopoly Cave disappeared; recent excavations in the Shore Temple Mahabalipuram (Seven Pagodas) have brought to light a Pallavagrandha inscription of Rajasimha—Narasimhavarman II—the builder of the Kailasanada Temple at Kanchipuram, to whom also we owe the Pallava pillars at Tirupporur and Vayalur, the latter of which contains an interesting genealogical record. Narasimhavarman I delighted in the titles of Chaityakari —temple-builder and Vatapikonda Narasimha—the Narasimha who took Vatapi—and probably the Rathas at Mahabalipuram were begun during his reign. He seems to have renewed the grant to the Mûlastâna temple at Tirukkalukunram which had been made by his ancestor Skanda Sishya. The temple at Triplicane in Madras has as an inscription in Pallavagrandha characters, a fact which attests to the antiquity of the capital of the so-called benighted presidency. The inscription of the Kudumiyamalai temple in Pallavagrandha characters is, so to say, a treatise on Hindu music. The East and West Gopuras of the Chidambaram temple were richly decorated by a Pallava, who as an insurance for his prospects in the world to come, used the goods obtained in this world for embellishing the inner walls with fine specimens of images in various poses and attitudes assumed by those who practice the art of dancing which is being forgotten altogether in South India. These figures which are more than a hundred in number have verses in Grandha characters inscribed over each explanatory of the posture. The sculptures accompanying the damaged epigraph in the Vaikunthaperumal temple, Kanchipuram, were evidently intended to illustrate real historic events connected with the succession of Nandivarman on the death of Parameswara II. I could easily add to the list, but the temples and inscriptions I have referred to are enough to give one an idea of the part played by the Pallava kings between the fifth and eighth centuries of the Christian era in Southern India.

The cave temples of the Pallavas were the natural successors of the earliest lithic monuments of the Tamil country, the Panchava beds already referred to. The practice of so fitting caves and caverns as to satisfy human needs by architecturally improving them first adopted by the Northern Buddhists was improved upon by the Pallavas. But the figures carved and the subjects illustrated by their architecture were from the Hindu Puranic Pantheon, without any particular leaning either to the Vaishnava or Saiva cult, the figures of Brahma, Vishnu and Siva appearing side by side in some of the Pallava temples. They seem to have been patrons of literature and of the fine arts. It is not usual here or elsewhere that we find a treatise on music or the art of dancing inscribed on stone. They bogan as Buddhists and gradually gave adherence to the Puranic faith.

The published grants generally begin by recounting the origin of the race from the lotus navel of Vishnu and bring the succession to the mythical Pallava who was nurtured in a litter of tender sprouts. Thereafter they give a genealogy which if partly based on tradition is in the main of historic value.

A plain narrative of a succession of events was evidently an impossible achievement for the State poet who composed the ordinary South Indian inscription. This is one of the disconcerting factors in South Indian epigraphical studies. A Dravidian people whose vernacular was Telugu or Tamil must have their inscriptions in unspoken Sanskrit. The more modern, the less familiar the language of the inscription. Every new race of kings on attaining prominence desired to trace its origin to the sun and the moon, the heroes of the Mahabarata or a supernatural being. And versifiers were not wanting who could shed a halo round the crowned head of a hero. The student of history has to reckon with such recurring attitudes of mind and corresponding creations of the imagination in studying South Indian inscriptions, which lay claim to trace the genealogy of the kings under whose auspices they were issued. Imagination and tradition acted and re-acted on each other. As a result we have a delicious jumble of tradition embellished by the poets' fancy. These remarks are suggested by the study of the inscriptions which pretend to give an apparently true account of the doings of a king whose religious benefaction is the immediate provocation for the composition of a seemingly historic narrative of hoary ancestry and hereditary greatness. These considerations are true of almost every South Indian inscription. All the more reason why earnest workers in the field of epigraphy should train themselves to separate fiction from fact and attempt to understand the true significance of what sometimes may be found expressed in tropes so dear to the heart of the State poet who composed the inscription.

By the time of Samudragupta's invasion of South India in the fourth century A.D., the Pallavas had their capitals in the three different provinces. That great monarch after his successful compaigns North, East, South and West had his achievements recorded on a stone pillar set up by Asoka six centuries previously at Allahabad. Of the many chieftains vanquished by him are mentioned Hastivarman of Vengi; Vishnugopa, king of Kanchi; and a third chieftain, Ugrasena of Palakkat. The Sanskrit charters issued from Dasanapura, Palakkuda and Menmadura in the fifth and sixth centuries do not throw much light on early Pallava history. From about the end of the sixth century, however, we have something more than mere conjecture to go upon. Simhavisnu the first king of whom we have some definite information claims to have defeated the Singhalese king of Ceylon as well as the Chera, Chola and Pandya. Synchronous almost with the prominence of the Pallavas under Simhavishnu was their hostile contact with the rising Chalukya power, a hostility which was destined eventually to put an end to Pallava supremacy in South India. To Simhavishnu's son, Mahendravarman (A. D. 600—625) we owe probably many of the monolithic cave temples in the North Arcot, Chingleput, South Arcot and Trichinopoly Districts with inscriptions giving one or other of his surnames. A Thondaiman who had the wealth, power and importance to have brought into existence so many works of art and was probably responsible for some of the Rathas of the deservedly admired Seven Pagodas should have been a monarch of no mean pretensions. His territories must have extended as far South as the Trichinopoly District. The accoutrements and adornments of the figures carved in the cave temples furnish an index as to the prosperity of his subjects and their cultural advancement.

He was succeeded by Narasimhavarman (A. D. 625—645), the conqueror of Vatapi. The Pallava power attained its zenith during his reign. He became practically the lord of Southern India, ruled over a territory which according to Hieun Thsang, who visited Kanchi during his reign, was about a thousand miles in circuit and assumed the title of Mahammalla.

The Velurpalayam plates referred to in the Government Epigraphist report for 1910-11 is typical of the grants from which we can construct a history of the Pallavas. "Kalabhartri, who may perhaps be the same as Kanagopa of other inscriptions is the first king mentioned. He is stated to have been the jewel of his race. His son was Chutapallava. From whom was born Virakurcha who acquired all the emblems of royalty on marrying the daughter of a Naga Princess. Then came Skanda Sishya who received the burden of maintaining the *ghatika* of Brahman from King Satya Sena. After him was born Kumarakrishna who took the town of Kanchi; and then came Buddhavarman 'the submarine fire to the ocean of Chola forces.' Here comes a break in the succession and we are informed that several kings including Vishnugopa passed away before a certain Hastivarman (I) was born. The king, it is stated, caused, by the favour of

Siva, the king of serpents named Drishti Visha to dance. After him came Simha Varma of great prowess and from him was born the victorious Simhavishnu who conquered the Chola territory which was resplendent with areca groves, was decorated by forests of paddy flats and sanctified by the (waters of the) daughter of Kavera (the Cauvery) "After this the geneology is on firmer ground. And the royal pedigree from about the end of the sixth century A.D. is brought down to the end of the eighth century of the same era." I have but set down the contents of a typical inscription in the words of Mr. Krishna Sastri. The conquest of Kanchi, the marriage with a Naga princess and the defeat of the Chola king are all facts of significance. The names, Skanda Sishya, Buddhavarman and Vishnugopa indicate an evolution in their religious faith. But further research alone must throw light on such matters.

The coins attributable to the Pallavas are all illustrative of the age for which we have also the aid of inscriptions and have to be ascribed to a period later than the sixth century. The emblems ordinarily appearing on the coins of the Pallavas are "the bull" and "the two-masted ship." A lion or lioness takes the place of the bull on the obverse of some coins. Some of them bear legends read by Dr. Hultzsch as Sri Bhara (Mahendravarman) Srinidhi (Rajasimha) Manapara. On the reverse of the coins appear one or other of the following emblems :—the Swastika, the sacrificial lamp, the chakram, the bow, the fish, the umbrella, the chaitya, the horse, the lion, the chank, the sacred vase and other emblems often occurring on the Andhra coinage. The coins are die-struck and well executed and occur in copper and silver; gold coins I have not met with. The appearance of the two-masted ship, as in the Andhra coins, indicates that the Pallavas had a maritime trade from the ports of the Coromandel coast. The emblems though of Buddhist origin seem to have been adopted by the Pallavas, in imitation of the Andhras; though the Pallava sculptures illustrate the Puranic Hindu Pantheon. I have published a tentative list of these coins, but the field of Pallava coinage has not been sufficiently explored and a people who built so many temples and wielded great power over many centuries must have struck a greater variety and a larger number of coins than I have come across. A systematic search for these in the Coast Districts is sure to increase our knowledge of the coinage of this ancient dynasty of kings. The bull as an emblem continues on the later Pandya and Chola coinage. The ancient Pandyan emblem (the fish), the Chola emblem (the tiger), and the Chera emblem (the bow) could all be traced to the symbolism of Buddhist times.

There is something like morphology in numismatics. There is a very intimate connection traceable between all the series of coins from the old punch marked, the old Madura, the Andhra and Pallava coins. They all bear Buddhist emblems, but the most recent of them do not use them as largely as the Andhras. There is also a gradual development in the form and the fabric of the coinage and some of the specimens from the Pallava period are as good as the issues of the present day mints.

I have given a very brief outline of the results achieved by a study of the coins and inscriptions of one of the darkest periods of South Indian history. Our knowledge has substantially increased. At various periods from the third century B. C. till the eighth century A. D., we are enabled by inscriptions, coins and contemporary literature to trace the history of South India with some precision. Many lacunæ must be allowed to remain in the chronology of the Andhras and the Pallavas till further evidence is forthcoming. If South India has been from various causes immune from the invasions and incursions which Hindustan experienced from before and since the time of Alexander the Great, South India history has been likewise free from scientific investigation. As the late Professor Sundaram Pillai pointed out, India proper is still 'Peninsular India' the India South of the Vyndhyas. "Here the bulk of the people continue distinctly to retain their pre-Aryan features, their pre-Aryan languages, their pre-Aryan social institutions. Even here the process of Aryanization has gone indeed too far to leave it easy for the historian to distinguish the native warp from the foreign woof. But if there is anywhere any chance of such successful disentanglement, it is in the South; and the further South we go to the larger does the chance grow."

I hope to take another opportunity of presenting before you a brief account of what has been achieved to lift the veil overhanging the history of South India, by the inscriptions and coins of Chalukyas, Pandyas and Cholas.

The Chalukyas and their Coinage

I

The Chalukyas with whose coinage I propose to deal here were the contemporaries of their inveterate foes, the Pallavas and the Cholas of the South. Overthrowing the Chalukyas the Cholas established a Viceroyalty in Vengi, the old Andhra country, the Vengorashtra of the grant of Pallava Raja Simhavarman and the Vengainaidu of Ko Raja Rajakesarivarman's Tamil Inscription. This was brought about quite as much by intermarriage between the two royal houses as by conquest.

Who were the Chalukyas and what part did they play in the history of the Dekkhan? These questions I shall attempt to answer by an account compiled from existing sources of information. This will enable us to follow the numismatics of the period from the fall of the Andhras up to the 12th century A. D.

The Chalukyas loom into prominence about the middle of the 6th century A. D. in Western and Southern India. Their first King, Pulakesin I, established his power about A. D. 550 in the territory surrounding Badami (Vatapi) in the modern Bijapur District. His possessions were extended by his sons Kirtivarman I and Mangalisa. The former conquered the Kadambas of Banavasi, the Mauryas of the Konkan and the Nalas in probably the modern districts of Bellary and Kurnool. The latter in addition to further successes in the Konkan, conquered towards the north, the Kalachuri King Buddha and by so doing acquired the northern parts of the Bombay Presidency.

One of Kirtivarman's sons ascended the throne of Vatapi as Pulakesin II in A. D. 608. He extended the Chalukya territory in every direction and made himself master of 'Vengi Desa' in the east, between the Krishna and the Godaveri and established his brother Kubja Vishnu Vardhana there as viceroy in the beginning of the 7th century A. D. This King sometime afterwards, probably in A. D. 632, by a formal division or by an act of rebellion, set up as an independent sovereign, in Pishtapura, the modern Pittapur as his capital; and founded the eastern Chalukya line which lasted till 1070 A. D. and became then absorbed into the Chola-Chalukya line.

The Western Chalukyas of Badami, the original stock, held their kingdom until a little more than half way through the 8th century. They then succumbed to the Rashtrakutas and the family remained in obscurity for over two hundred years. The dynasty was restored to power by Taila II in A.D. 973. His successors held sovereignty for over two centuries more and then the Chalukyas sank into obscurity and finally disappeared.

Pulakesin II describes himself as of the family of "the Chalukyas who are glorious: who are of the Manavyagotra which is praised throughout the whole world; who are Haritiputras: who have been nourished by the Seven Mothers who are the Seven Mothers of mankind: who have acquired an uninterrupted continuity of prosperity through the favour and protection of Kartikeya and who have had all kings made subject to them at the sight of the *boar-crest* which they acquired through the favour of the divine *Narayana* (Vishnu)".

The Chalukya crest was the "*Varaha lanchchana.*" Their banner was the "*Palidhvaja.*" They also adopted the insignia of the Signs of the rivers, Ganga and Yamuna.

They were votaries of Vishnu in his incarnation as a boar; but nevertheless they displayed a praiseworthy tolerance in matters of religion patronising the Jainas and Saivas equally with the followers of *Narayana.*

In later times there was gradually evolved a legendary history of the origin of the Chalukyas from Brahma as born from the lotus that grew from Vishnu's navel and, as Dr. Fleet observes, much of this account seems to be a farrago of vague legend and Puranic myths of no authority, devised about the 10th century A. D.—at about the time when all the great families were looking up their pedigrees and devising more or less fabulous genealogies.

Chalukyan history divides itself primarily into that of the western or the original stock of Badami, and of the eastern Chalukyas of Vengi.

The Western Chalukyas have two distinct periods, that of the early Chalukyas of Badami and that of the later of Kalyani, the Rashtrakutas having, as above pointed out, ruled over the territories of the Western Chalukyas wrested from Kirtivarman II, "turning the boar into a deer," that is to say, putting the

Chalukya forces to flight. The Rashtrakuta rule continued till the fallen fortunes of the Chalukyas were restored under Taila II.

The information available from copper plate grants and lithic records has been collected by Dr. Fleet in his Canarese dynasties and Dr. Ramakrishna Gopal Bhandarkhar in his Early History of the Dekkhan. The large number of inscriptions brought to light after their time of research do not materially alter the general outline traced by these scholars.

Among the kings of the Western Chalukyas of Badami, Pulakesin II appears to have been the greatest. His full title was Satyasraya Sri Prithivi Vallabha Maharaja. He ruled from A.D. 611 and his career of conquest closed before A.D. 634. Hiuen Tsiang, the Chinese pilgrim, describes the prince in the following terms:—"He is of the race of Tsa-ta-li (Kshatriya). His name is Pu-lo-ki-she; his ideas are large and profound and he extends widely his sympathy and benefactions. His subjects serve him with perfect devotion."

In the 36th year of Koshru II of Persia (A.D. 591 to 628) letters and presents were exchanged between him and Pulakesin; the Ajanta cave painting depicting the presentation of a letter from a Persian king to an Indian king probably refers to this interesting incident. His younger brother, Vishnu Vardhana, otherwise called Vishamasiddhi, was first appointed viceroy over the Satara and Pandarpur districts in the Bombay Presidency and then obtained as adumbrated already the province of Vengi between the Lower Krishna and Godavari where he founded the branch of the Eastern Chalukyas. Pulakesin's second brother Jayasimha seems to have been viceroy of Nasik; Pulakesin's eldest son, of the Savantvada district, and another son Aditya Varman of a province near the confluence of the Krishna and the Tungabhadra. All these facts are established by inscriptions.

In 634 A. D. the Pallava Narasimha Varman I attacked Pulakesin II and laid waste the western Chalukya capital, Badami. But his son Vikramaditya I. on the back of his horse Chitrakantha with sword in hand, came off victorious in battle; he defeated Narasimha Varman I. and Narendra Varman and surpassed Parameswara Varman in statesmanship and thus bruised and crushed the Kshatryas—conquering Iswara Pota Raja. He took Kanchi, 'whose huge walls were insurmountable and hard to be broken; which was surrounded by a large moat that was unfathomable and hard to be crossed and resembled the girdle (Kanchi) of the southern region.' He was ably assisted by his son Vinayaditya and grandson Vijayaditya. They brought to subjection the Malavas, Cholas, Pandyas, and Kalabhras and thus Vikramaditya became again the paramount sovereign of the country between the three seas: that is of the peninsula of India.

Vinayaditya, A. D. 680-694, known as Satyasrya Rajasriya and 'Yuddha Malla' came to the throne after the death of Vikramaditya. He seems to have, between the 11th and 14th years of his reign, succeeded in making the Pallavas, Cholas and Pandyas his allies. He acquired the *Palidhwaja* banner, by defeating a northern king and levied tribute from Ceylon. He likewise acquired the signs of the Yamuna and Ganga and the Dakka (the drum). Grants of his are found in many places in Western Dekkhan as well as in the modern Bellary and Kurnool Districts and Mysore.

The next king of note before the downfall of the early Chalukyas was Vikramaditya II (733 A. D.) He marched against the Pallava capital of Kanchi and defeating the Pallava prince, did not destroy the city ; on the other hand he helped to restore the endowments of the Rajasimheswara temple. He attacked and reduced the Cholas, Keralas and the Pandyas.

After this king, the early Chalukya line waned and the Rashtrakuta Krishna Raja alias *Akalavarsha*, 760 A. D., is spoken of "as having, with the aid of the Gods in the form of his counsellors or followers, churned the ocean of the Chalukya race which had been resorted to by mountains in the shape of kings afraid of their ways of power being destroyed—an ocean that was inaccessible to others—and drawn out from it the Lakshmi of paramount Sovereignty." This was the Krishnaraja who presented to posterity the "Kailasa" in Elur, described by the sculptor himself as "the temple of Siva self-existent: for, such beauty is not to be found in a work of art."

The Rashtrakutas were powerful princes and their rock-cut temples attest to their greatness. The Puranic religion flourished under them and they were great patrons of literature. Jainism still held the prominence which it had under the early Chalukyas if it did not make greater progress. They all assumed the title of *Sri Vallabha*.

As already indicated Taila II restored the power of the Chalukya sovereigns in the Western Dekkhan. This happened in A. D. 973-974: and the event is described in an inscription of Vikramaditya VI (1077-1125 A D.) :—

" Om : Hail, in the lineage of Soma—there is the glorious Chalukya race, which is the abode of truth, liberality, heroism and other virtuous qualities and has destroyed the races of hostile kings simply by the quickness of its bannered armies. In that race,

to Vikramaditya IV, who was accounted the favourite of fortune and the favourite of the goddess of victory over enemies and to Bontha Devi who resembled the goddess ' Sri ' there was born a son King Taila II;

having first plucked and destroyed some Rattas; having killed the radiant Munja; having by the terror of the pride of his arm taken the head of Panchala in battle; and having possessed himself of the regal dignities of the Chalukyas—Taila, unaided, caused the whole circuit of the earth to be considered free from troubles for 24 years, beginning with the year Srimukha."

The later Chalukyas, unlike the earlier ones who delighted in the title Srivallabha, assumed titles like Tribhuvana Malla, A.D. 1009, Jagadekamalla, A.D. 1016, Trailokyamalla, A. D. 1149, Ahavamalla, A. D. 1042, Bhuvanekamalla A. D. 1075, Yuddhamalla A. D. 1125- and Bhulokamalla.

Someswara I, A.D. 1042, Ahavamalla and Vikramaditya Tribhuvanamalla were the most noteworthy of the later Chalukya Princes.

Someswara assumed the titles of Ahavamalla and Trailokyamalla and as usual with the Chalukya princes turned his arms against the Cholas. He then marched against Dhara, the capital of Bhoja and captured it. This hostility with the king of Malva was perhaps an inheritance from Tailapa who had caused Munja to be put to death. The tradition recorded in the Bhoja Charitram must have been correct to this extent that to avenge his uncle's death the king of Malva formed a confederacy with some neighbouring princes and attacked the dominions of the Chalukyas. This confederacy, perhaps it was, that Someswara I successfully broke. He then directed his attention to the countries on the Western coast, and to commemorate his operations erected a triumphal arch there, proceeding by the seashore to the extreme south of the Peninsula. In his progress through that part of the country, the Chola king attacked him but was defeated. Someswara thereupon proceeded to his capital, Kanchi, which he captured and the Chola king had to flee for his life.

Ahavamalla's operations against Bhoja and the Cholas are alluded to in an inscription and he is also represented to have fought with the king of Kanya Kubja or Kanouj and compelled him to betake himself to the cavern of mountains for safety. He founded the city of Kalyana and made it his capital.

Of his three sons the ablest was Vikramaditya. He was deputed to invade the Sunda country or Bengal and Kamarupa or Assam. He conquered the Keralas. The King of Sinhalas submitted on his approach. Then he took the City of Gangaikonda Chola and proceeded to the country of the Cholas, the prince of which fled and took refuge in the mountains. Vikramaditya then entered Kanchi and plundered it and thence directed his march to Vengi and to Chakrakota.

While Vikramaditya was so employed Ahavamalla was seized with a strong fever. When he observed his end approaching, he caused himself to be taken to the banks of the Tungabhadra. He bathed in the water of the river and gave away a great deal of gold in charity. Then entering the river again he proceeded until the water reached his neck, and in the din caused by the waves and a number of musical instruments drowned himself in A.D. 1069, thus attaining "Jalasamadhi." Ahavamalla, according to Bilhana, performed a great many sacrifices and was very liberal to men of learning. On account of his virtues poets made him the hero of the later poems and dramas composed by them.

Vikramaditya hadto wage a fratricidal war against his brother Someswara II before he could ascend his father's throne. Someswara forming an alliance with the Chola prince Rajiga, attacked Vikramaditya who after considerable hesitation proceeded to crush his brother. He ascended the throne in 1076 A.D. He had a long and peaceful reign of fifty years. He assumed the name of *Tribhuvanamalla* and is known by the names of *Kalivikrama* and *Parmaderaya*. He abolished the Saka Era and established his own, but it fell into disuse not long after his death. In the latter part of his reign he had to repel the invasion of his dominions by the Hoysala prince, Vishnu Vardhana. Vikramaditya was a patron of learning. Bilhana and Vignaneswara, both benefited by his patronage.

It is beyond the purpose of this brief notice of the history of the later Chalukyas to go into further detail about the doings of the other princes of the line. It is to follow the numismatics of this period that I have recounted this short outline of Chalukya history gathered from various sources.

The Kalachuris occupied their dominions; and then sovereigns assuming the titles of *Bujabala Malla, Ahavamalla,* 1156 A. D. *Nissamka malla,* 1183 A. D. and *Viranarayana,* continued to assert themselves in the southern Dekkhan till about the end of 12th century A. D. I have dealt thus with the original stock of Chalukyas, the western branch of Badami and their immediate successors during the two periods of their sway in the Dekkhan.

From time to time inscriptions referring to the early Chalukya kings of Vatapi and the later Kings of Kalyan have been found in the Ceded Districts. A copper plate grant of Vikramaditya I (655-680) mentions his victorious camp at Pampatirtha.

One of the earliest records found in the Bellary district is that of Ahava Malla (Nurmadi Taila II) A. D. 978, who expelled the Rashtrakutta king, Kokka II. Four years afterwards Aditya Varman renews a grant in the Bellary District. But no inscriptions of Vikramaditya V, and Satyasraya seem to have been found in this District; apparently the Chola Raja Raja just about their reigns successfully attacked the Chalukyas. But as the Chola could not permanently regulate the affairs of the acquired territory from his distant capital, the Chalukyas established themselves again in these districts in Jayasimha's time.

The Eastern Chalukya dynasty founded by Vishnuvardhana Vishama Siddhi, continued its uninterrupted sway for nearly five centuries till it was finally absorbed into the Chola line.

Most of the Eastern Chalukya grants have been examined and a complete genealogy is now available tracing the succession from the time of the founder, Vishnu Vardhana-Vishama Siddhi, to that of Virachoda Vishnu-Varadhana IX; that is, for a period of more than five centuries.

A grant of *Vira Choda*, almost the very last in this genealogical table is inscribed on five copper plates obtained from the Karnam of Chellur in the Cocanada Taluk of the Godavari District. They are held together in a ring, which however is not whole in its present condition. The plates belonged to Sir W. Elliott and are in the British Museum. The ring bears a seal resting on a cast representation of an expanded lotus flower bearing on its surface on a countersunk surface the legend "Sri Bhuvanankusah"; over the legend, there appears the figure of a boar which faces the right and is flanked by two lamps, two *chamaras*, the symbols of the Sun and the Moon, an elephant goad and a conch. Below the legend is a *dammaka* (drum): an expanded lotus flower, and emblems representing the *Makara torana* and a *Swastika*. The grant is a typical one and is an epitome of the history of the Eastern Chalukya dynasty from its origin till the time of the donor and incidentally refers to the connection between the Dravidian Cholas and Eastern Chalukya Kings of Vengi.

The Vamsavali of the inscription consists of four parts:—The first gives the mythical account of fifty-nine emperors, of the Lunar race supposed to have reigned in Ayodhya. The second deals with five early Chalukya kings ending with Kirtivarman. The third sets out the succession of the Eastern Chalukyas of Vengi from Vishama Siddhi to Vimaladitya and the fourth furnishes us with an account of the later Eastern Chalukyas during their connection with the Cholas.

The son of Vimaladitya, Raja Raja, 1015-22 A. D., is said to have married Ammanga Devi, the daughter of Rajendra Chola of the Chola Race. Their son Rajendra Chola, the great Chola Emperor, Kulottunga Deva or Raja Narayana, at first ascended the throne of Vengi, conquered the Kerala, Pandya, Kuntala and other countries and was subsequently anointed in the Chola kingdom. He married Madurantaki, the daughter of a Rajendra Deva of the Solar race. When Kulottunga rose to be the Chola Emperor he had given the Vengi Kingdom to his paternal uncle, Vijayaditya, who died after a reign of fifteen years. Then (1022) he gave Vengi to his son—*Raja Raja* and when the latter had returned after one year's reign, to Raja's Raja's younger brother *Virachoda* who was crowned in Jagannanda Nagara.

The Chellur plates above referred to not only throw light on the connection between the Eastern Chalukyas of Vengi and the ancient Chola kings of the South but also furnish some important synchronisms illumining a portion of the history of the latter kingdom. The Leyden, 'grant' (so called because preserved in the University Museum of Leyden of Holland,) and other Tamil inscriptions of the Chola renaissance, refer to three Western Chalukya kings, as the antagonists of the Chola kings, Satyasraya, Jayasimha and Ahavamalla or Someswara I.

This comparison of the Chellur plates with the Leyden grant led to the realization of the common error of confounding the two Chola kings, Raja Raja and Rajendra Chola, with their Eastern Chalukya grandsons who seem to have taken the same names as their mothers' fathers. In reality the Eastern Chalukya king, Raja Raja I, ruled only over Vengi. His son Rajendra Choda *alias* Kulottunga Chola Deva I, A. D. 1063-1112, though at first king of Vengi, seems to have inherited the Chola kingdom from his father-in-law, the Chola Rajendra Deva.

I have given the above brief outline of the Eastern Chalukya history from the time of their rise in the middle of the 6th century till their downfall in the 11th century, in order to enable me to interest you in the numismatic evidence relating to the period.

The Western Chalukyas of Vatapi and Kalyani ruled as we have seen over the whole of the table-land between the Nerbudda and the Krishna together with the coast of the Bay of Bengal from Ganjam to Nellore for about five centuries. So abiding was their influence that the indigenous gold currency in South India was permanently impressed with the standard adopted by them. Among the symbols employed on South Indian Coins, the most celebrated was the 'varaha' or the boar. Vishnu in his 'varaha Avatara' or incarnation of the boar, was the family deity of the Chalukyas. The Chalukya Kings of the Western and Eastern branches adopted the figure of the boar on their seals and claimed to have obtained the same through the special favour of Narayana or Vishnu. It was not only impressed on the gold coins weighing between 52 to 68 grains of the Chalukyas of Vatapi and Kalyani but was also adopted by the Rayas of Vijaiyanagar and the Pandyas of Madura and is said to have been used by petty local chiefs in the Carnatic. The gold coins of the above weight whether issued by the Chalukyas, Vijaiyanagar Rayas or the various East India Companies or the Muhammadan states of the South, were still popularly known as 'Varahas', even though they had not on them the figure of the boar, but had representations from the Hindu Pantheon of Siva and Parvati, Krishna or Venkatesa or only the mint dates and proper names of Muhammadan kings.

Notwithstanding the permanent mark left thus on South Indian coinage by the 'Varaha' coins of the Chalukyas, and the long period during which the two branches exerted their sway in South India, the specimens available from their time do not illustrate more than the reigns of a few of the numerous princes whose names have been definitely fixed by inscriptions. This paucity of numismatic evidence is not peculiar to the Chalukyas alone. It is the characteristic feature of the history of the coinage of the three great Dravidian kingdoms of the South. The Pallavas whose history has been built up mainly with the aid of inscriptions, have left us but a few specimens of their coinage. The Cholas and Chalukyas have left magnificient examples of their architecture; but very few of 'their varahans' and 'tankas', 'pons' and 'madais' have survived them. After each successful invasion or war, and there were many of them during the past ten centuries, vast quantities of gold must have been carried away as booty. The coins so removed must have been melted and converted into the currency of the State to which they had been conveyed. In the troublous period following the disintegration of the indigenous sovereignties, the habit must have grown of concealing what was left, from the sudden incursions of enemies. When the coins ceased to be current for a very long time naturally they were probably thrown in the melting pot to be used as jewellery or converted into coins of the reigning power. Thus it is now reserved to the ploughman, the well-digger or the action of time and rain to bring the hidden treasure to light. One such hoard of 20,000 gold pieces was recently discovered in Kodur in the Nellore District. These are bound to be of great value to the study of the numismatics of the period I am dealing with. They are now being examined by the Government Epigraphist.

Situated as we are, it is best to know what has already been unearthed and identified leaving further finds to add to our knowledge.

The earliest coins known in the Dekhan are spherules of gold with a symbol punched on them. Then follow a hoard of eldlings found in the Konkan with the figure of a lion superimposed on the earlier punch marks. The *padma* or the lotus flower takes the central place around which are separately punched various marks, two of which are the Kanarese letter Sri. A still different variety has a conch (turbnella rapa) with a weapon opposite to it incused on the gold piece. A gold *padmatanka* irregularly concave and cup-shaped, has a well-executed representation of the Padma; and the legend 'Sri' in Canarese above and below. A well-executed 'conch', in the right '*p*.,' a nagari legend: *ra* and *ma* (?) are visible. Frequently the chank and the bow appear together. Coins are also found with the figure of Hanuman, the lion, or the figure of Krishna playing on the flute. Those with the *padma* or lotus flower surrounded by four punch-marked lions are however more numerous than the rest.

The *padma* is sometimes superseded by a *swastika* which appears on certain specimens as the chief and central emblem. These symbols give way on other specimens to a central lion, surrounded by four lions and four other symbols or characters making eight in all, covering the whole of the obverse, the reverse being plain. Along with punch-marked coins, die-struck coins also seem to have been current in which a single lion with an ornamental circular border, occupies the obverse and the reverse has a floral design, seen on the so-called Gajapati varahas.

The reverse of all these coins is convex in shape and is found often punched with various seals like the bow, the elephant, the chaitya and other symbols peculiar to the period of transition from Buddhism to Puranic Hinduism.

All or any of these coins cannot be attributed with any certainty to the Chalukyas. The lion was the emblem of the Kadambas and the *padma* (lotus) seems to have been adopted by them on their coinage.

The Chalukyas who hailed from the North-West were the natural successors of the Kadambas. We first see the boar taking the place of the *padma* or lotus on coins which we can with any certainty attribute to the Cahalukyas. The punch-marked coinage of the Chalukyas with their dynastic device, the Boar, accompanied by legends in large Halakanada characters, each character being impressed by a separate punch, still persisted till a late period. Sir W. Elliott seems to have assumed that punch-marked coins ceased to be in vogue about the fifth or sixth century A. D. But we find such coins in the times of the later Eastern Chalukya Kings. The issue of punch-marked coins was occasionally revived long after the time when the use of the die had been fully introduced.

Let me first give you a description of a few of these coins which cannot be ascribed to any sovereign definitely.

A gold coin, weighing about 65 grains, has on its obverse a boar to left with the sun and moon and part of a scroll above, a scroll below, possibly representing the Yamuna and Ganga, and also a device which may be the *Palidhwaja.* On the reverse there is a floral design, which is repeated at various periods on South Indian coinage and thus has given the name of *Phuli hun or flowery pon* to many South Indian gold coins.

On the reverse of gold coins, with the figure of the boar on the obverse appears a radiating chakram or wheel; or lion; a *sankam* or conch shell; or a lion looking backwards.

We have as yet only three types of coins which could be attributed specifically to a Sovereign and these belong to the later period of 'Kalyani.'

Gold coins weighing about 58 grains with, on the obverse, nine punch-marks, of which five represent a lion, two the syllable Sri, one the word 'Jaya' and the remaining the word 'Deva' must be attributed to Jayasimha II.

The second set of coins, is that of *Jagadekamalla*, 1016-1040 A.D.

Obverse :—Concave in shallow cup shape; temple in centre; seven punch-marks in margin *viz.*, three of 'Sri' and four of the characters *Jagadekamalla*, A.D. 1016.

The third variety is described by Dr. Hultzsch as follows :—

Obverse :—Nine punch-marks of which five represent lions, two the syllable Sri, one 'Trele' and one 'Malla.'

(Someswara I Trailokya Malla 1042)

The reverse is in each case blank. Of much the same type as these specimens are the dozen or more varieties of the 20,000 gold pieces of the Kodur find already referred to. By the courtesy of Rao Saheb Krishna Sastri, I was enabled to make a cursory examination of the distinct varieties selected by him. Some of these types were dealt with by Sir W. Elliot in his Numismatic Gleanings, a contribution to this Society's Journal in 1858. Similar pieces are in the collections of Dewan Bahadur T. M. Ranga Chariar and myself. Sir W. Elliot in his contribution to the Numismatica Orientalia figures coins of this type as Nos. 10, 13 to 16, and 20 in Plate I and No. 60, 66 and and 67 in plate II. He obtained most of them from the Southern Mahratta Country. In the imperfect state of South Indian Numismatic studies fifty years ago he attributed them all to the Kadamba Dynasty. But having regard to the same type of coins prevailing so late as the 12th century as shown with reference to the coins of Jayasimha, Jagadekamalla and Trailokya malla, the coins of the Nellore find probably belong to the Western Chalukyas of Kalyani or the Rashtrakutas who preceded them or the Kalachuri commander of forces Bijjala and his successors who overthrew the Western Chalukyas of Kalyani.

Sir Walter Elliot's No. 66 plate II is described by him as follows:—

Gold: Weight 54·8 grains: From Sunda. Obv: Indistinct figure of a lion in the centre with four punch marks, two being the word 'Sri'; the third a word which has been read as *Bhujam* (?) Rev: plain.

His No. 10 has the words 'Sri' as well as the word V*ijaya*.

The legend 'Bhuja' is very suggestive. The usurpation of the Chalukya throne was achieved by the Chalukya general of the Kalachuri Vamsa, named Bijjala, who assumed the title of Bhuja Bala Chakravarti. The legend on the latter coin reminds one of the prince who assumed the title of Vijaya Siddhi. The Government Epigraphist in his latest report, records an inscription of Bhuja Bala Chakravarti issued within two or three years of his usurpation. Bhuja Bala perhaps took the prevailing type of coins in the dominions of the Western Chalukyas and impressed his title thereon. If the surmise be correct we have to trace the monarchs who issued the coins of this type to a much later period than that of the Kadamba Dynasty.

Of the eight varieties in the Kodur find I saw with Rao Saheb Krishna Sastri, one could be certainly attributted to Jagadekamalla. The rest divide themselves into two classes, those with the 'Padma' and those with the lotus or the lion as their characteristic device. Those with the lion symbol have the syllables *yana* or *Jaga* or *Kata* while those with the *padma* have the legends *Bhuvana*, *Avani*, *Bhujavira* or *Yada*. I have not been able to carefully study the legends or the arrangements of the various symbols on the coins in question; but my impression as one who has tried to decipher old coins for more than a quarter of a century is that the coins all belong to the period of the later Western Chalukyas of Kalyani or their successors in this portion of the Dekkhan.

The Eastern Chalukya Dynasty had its own coinage. The first King, Kubja Vishnuvardhana (A. D. 615—633) seems to have issued coins in gold, silver and copper. A *varaha* of the type of Padmatanka has a *Nagari* legend reading 'Sidhi'—standing for Vishama Siddhi, the title assumed by the founder of the Eastern Chalukya Dynasty. Base silver coins of the same king are described in the Cataloguo of the Indian Museum as follows:—

Obverse:—Within a dotted border a rude lion to the right; Telugu legend above Vishama Siddhi (successful in scaling inaccessible places.)

Reverse:—Within a border of rays double trident, surmounted by a crescent and flanked by two lamps.

Seventyone specimens in copper in the Madras Museum have the same devices on the obverse and the reverse and the legend in Canarese, Vishama

Siddhi. The next King represented by an extant coin is Saktivarman or Chalukya Chandra, whose gold Varahan has the following obverse:—

In the centre a boar to right under an umbrella, fly whisk on each side: a lamp in front of and another behind the animal, old Canarese legend "Sri Chalukya Chandra, Sa: 13. (Year 13 of the reign). This Eastern Chalukya King who ruled over the Kingdom of Vengi for 12 years from 1000 to 1012 A. D. is mentioned by his proper name Saktivarman in the Chellur grant as well as by his secondary name of Chalukya Chandra.

It is curious that these coins were found outside India in the island of Ramri off the Coast of British Burma separated from the mainland by Arakkan. Specimens were also found in Siam. The following tradition recounted by Dr. Fleet in the Indian Antiquary for March 1890 attempts to account for the occurrence of these coins in places so far removed from the Vengi country as Ramri and Cheduba.

During the reign of a King of Arakkan he wanted to have a gold image of Buddha set up. He asked for contributions in metal for fashioning the image from various Kings. Some Kings brought their contributions in person and in seven metals; gold, silver, brass, copper etc., and the image was made which is said to be now in Mandalay. Those who did not reach the place in time, not wishing to return home with the offerings intended for so sacred an object buried in the ground the metals which they had taken with them as religious offerings.

Of the Eastern Chalukya King, Raja Raja, who reigned from A. D. 1022 to 1063 are two gold varahans weighing each 66½ grains. In the centre stands a boar facing the proper left and surrounded by two lamps, an elephant goad, a parasol and two indistinct symbols which may be the sun and the moon. Below the boar's head is the Telugu letter *ja* in one case and in the other the letter *ka*. In the margin is the legend Sri Raja Sa: 34 or 37. The central device and each of the six portions of the marginal legend were struck by a separate punch. The punches show through on the plain reverse. The obverse is irregularly concave in shape and this condition was evidently caused by the gradual bending of the thin meta during the application of the six punches.

A gold fanam, 7·2 grains in weight, with a group of symbols generally found on the coins of the Chola Kings Uttama Chola, Rajendra Chola, Gangai Konda Chola to be dealt with presently under the coinage of the Cholas has on its obverse, a seated tiger, two fishes and the bow, respectively the Chola, Pandya, Chera emblems. On the reverse of the gold fanam is the Nagari legend Yuddhamalla. Yuddhamalla is the title of more than one King of the Eastern Chalukya Dynasty. In the pedigree prepared by Dr. Fleet, Yuddhamalla is shown as the son of Kali Vishnu Vardhana V. This Yuddhamalla had a grandson Yuddhamalla. Both these princes flourished much earlier than the Chola conquest of Vengi after which alone the group of symbols above referred to came in vogue on Chalukya-Chola coins. We have therefore to look to that period for the prince Yuddhamalla who issued the gold coin in question. Was there a period in which the Cholas held sway for thirty years and more in Vengi Nadu? Dr. Fleet seems to think that this period was later than what could be ascribed to the Yuddhamallas so far known.

Among the copper coins bearing the Pandyan emblem, the fish, and the Tamil legend "Sundara Pandya" are a variety which have on their obverse a standing boar, the Chalukyan emblem with the sun and the moon above the boar. During the constant conflict between the Cholas and Western Chalukyas in which each claimed to be victorious, the Chalukyas of Kalyani seem to have been friendly with the Pandyas, for we find the Chalukyas served by Pandyan feudatories or governors. The names of such governors have been noted by the Government Epigraphist from inscriptions copied by his department. These coins with the fish emblem of the Pandyan and the boar crest of the Chalukyas probably point to this connection between the Chalukyas and the Pandyas.

A unique coin from the Nellore District has on the obverse a standing figure in regal robes, the characteristic figure on the obverse of the coins of the great Chola King Raja Raja. On the reverse there appears the Chalukya emblem, the boar, with a Canarese legend, the first and last letter of which could alone be deciphered, Pra—pa, Pratapa (?) It apparently belongs to the period when the Chola and Eastern Chalukya were on equal terms, at any rate when the Cholas had no objection to the appearance of the dynastic device of the Chalukyas on the same coin with the Chola emblem on the obverse.

A number of fanams of the Eastern Chalukya period occur. They bear the symbol of the lion as on the coins of Trailokya Malla and Jayasimha. The lion appears on the coins of the Hoysalas and the Kadambas of Goa. But these fanams are of a distinctively Chalukya type with Canerese legends like the coins of Trailokyamalla.

I think I have brought together all the available information on the coinage of the Chalukyas. I shall now proceed to the Cholas and their coinage.

The Cholas and their Coinage.

Centuries before the Christian Era, the Cholas had established themselves on the coast of Coramandel (Chola Mandalam) and enjoyed a civilization not less advanced than that of the Aryan Settlements in the North. They were referred to along with the Keralas and the Pandyas in the Second Rock Edict of the Buddhist Emperor, Asoka, in the third century B. C. The great chronicle of Ceylon, an ancient work in Pali called the Mahavanso, made it the theme of one of its main episodes, the war waged against the Island by the Chola Tamils in the early centuries preceding the Christian Era.

The first capital of the Cholas was Uraiyur, probably the oldest portion of the modern Trichinopoly; and later on they ruled from their capital Jayam-Konda-Cholapuram, in the Udaiyarpalayam Taluk of the Trichinopoly district. Other places there are too in the same district, which remind us by their names of these ancient rulers, such as Gangai-Konda-Chola-puram and Gandaradittam. As the Chola kings grew in power they had as their capitals Tanjore, Kumbakonam and Conjivaram and had viceroys in Rajahmundry in the north and Madura in the south. Their principal port was Kaveripattinam near the northern mouth of the Kaveri. The Chola inscriptions and coins which have hitherto come to light relate to a period between the ninth and thirteenth centuries of the Christian era, during which the Cholas rose into great prominence and finally declined, leaving the numerous South Indian temples, inscriptions and coins to attest their greatness. Inscriptions are not wanting to show that the Cholas were a power to be reckoned with even anterior to the ninth century of the Christian era.

Between the ninth and thirteenth centuries of the Christian era the Chola Kings, with varying success, attempted to maintain their supremacy over the whole of the Southern Presidency. In order to understand the coins of this period it is necessary to bear in mind who were the contemporary kings who ruled in different portions of the country over which the Cholas struggled for predominence. They were the Western Chalukyas of Kalyani and the Eastern Chalukyas of Vengi in the north and the Pallavas who had ruled on the Coramandel coast with Kanchipuram as their capital. From Nellore and the Ghauts to the sea, was the ancient Dravida Desam, or the land of the Tamils, of which the northern portion, the Chola Desam, extended from the Kaveri to the Palar; from the Kaveri to Comorin was the Pandya country; and the Chera country comprised all the territory westward as far as the sea. Another race of Kings playing a prominent part in the Chola history of this period are the Gangas, who ruled probably from Mukhalingam near Parlakimedi in the Ganjam district. And if to these be added the Sinhalese sovereigns who governed the island of Ceylon, during the time of the Chola ascendancy in the mainland and the kings of Pegu, the tale of sovereignties, with the conquest of which the Chola history mainly deals, would be almost complete.

The large number of Chola Inscriptions copied by the Government Epigraphist's department has been reviewed from time to time, and Professor Krishnaswami Aiyangar has given some years ago a scholarly treatment to the evidence available for building up a history of the Cholas.

I shall, as in the case of the Chalukyas, merely indicate the chronology and succession established by epigraphical researches in order to enable me to deal with the coinage of the period. Parantaka ruled from A. D. 907 to 949 from Uraiyur and was known as 'Madurantaka' and 'Vira Narayana.' The Jains were numerically strong during his reign but he is also reputed to have built the Kanaka Sabha or the Golden Hall of the Chidambaram temple, a meritorious act of devotion to Siva, to which more than one Chola sovereign lays claim. No coins of the King have been yet found.

After Parantaka (whose accession was in A.D. 907 and death in A. D. 949) till we come to the time of his great grandson Raja Raja, who ascended the throne in A.D. 985, we meet with the name of no remarkable Chola King. 'Certain inscriptions of Parantaka are of special interest to the student of village institutions by reason of the full details they give of the manner in which local affairs were administered by well-organised local committees, or Panchayats, excercising administrative and judicial control under royal sanction.'

The immediate predecessor of Raja Raja was the grandson of Parantaka A. D. 907–49 and the son of Gandaraditya A. D, 956–7. He assumed the title of *Madurantaka* A.D. 969–70 and was known as *Uttama Chola.* To this monarch must be assigned one of the two varieties of coins, the gold *madai* bearing the legend 'Uttama Chola' in Grantha characters and having a seated tiger with a fish in front of it, the tiger being the dynastic emblem of the Cholas and the fish that of the Pandyas. It was not unnatural that the King who assumed the name 'Madurantaka' conqueror of the Pandyan capital Madura,' should adopt on his coins also the Pandyan emblem of the fish in token of his sovereignty over the Pandyan country. Chola inscriptions constantly refer to the Madurantaka Madai as a coin with reference to which the fineness and weight of other coins in gold had to be tested. The *madai* was probably equal to a *Kalanju* while the *panam* was equal to a *Manjadi.* The Rajarajankasu mentioned in the Chola inscriptions of Tanjore seems to have varied from ¾ to 15/16 of a Kalanju. The Kalanju *is* also said to be equal to a Krishnakanhi. The *mahsa* of Ceylon is said to be of the same weight as the *madai* of Madurantaka. There was also a silver currency. Indeed the coins with the legends, Rajendra, Uttama Chola, Gangai-konda Chola and Kulottunga Chola to be presently referred to are all silver *kasus.* 'Pon' and 'Kasu' are likewise used for gold coins in the Chola period. The other coin of Uttama Chola has the Chera emblem the bow, in addition to the fish and the tiger and has the legend in Devanagari characters and this coin has to be attributed to a later reign, that of Rajendra I whose coins bearing the same emblems have the legend in Nagari, 'Sri Rajendra.'

One unique specimen has the legend in old Tamil 'Avanipa Sekharan Cholaha,' with two fishes on the obverse but without any symbol to indicate that it had a Chola origin. Was it issued by a Pandyan King, Avanipa Sekharan Srivallabha mentioned in an inscription in the rock-cut temple at Sittana Vasal or was the coin that of a Chola of the period of the Chola ascendancy when they claimed to have conquered all their neighbours? In the *Indian Antiquary* for 1892, Dr. Hultzsch read the legend as 'Avanipa Sekaran Golaga,' and interpreted it to mean the round coin of 'Avanipa Sekaran,' but he was not quite certain of his reading. The absence of the dynastic emblem of the tiger is not peculiar to this coin alone, for, as will be presently pointed out, many of the coins of Raja Raja do not bear that emblem. It is not improbable that imitating the pronunciation of the Sanskrit 'Cholah' an attempt was made to transliterate the word in Tamil, in order that the legend might sound quite classical. It was unnecessary to show on the coin the Chola's dynastic emblem when the name of the king himself was given, while the two fishes on the obverse indicated his supremacy in the Pandyan and Chola territories. On the other hand reading the legend as 'Golaga' and interpreting it as a 'round coin' would lead to the assumption that the perfectly superfluous information that the coin was round in shape, was conveyed by the legend, when the roundness of the coin was an obvious index of its shape.

Copper coins with the legend, Kôdandaraman, have been discovered. Below umbrella-flanked chowries, the legend 'Kôdandaraman' in Tamil is found on the obverse: on the reverse below the crescent are two fishes separated by a sceptre.

Parantaka I had a son named 'Sri Kôdandaraman' and his inscriptions have been copied. Kôdandaraman is probably identical with Rajaditya.

After Madurantaka *alias* Uttama Chola, came by far the greatest of the Chola kings, Raja Raja I, *alias* Raja Kesari Varma who ascended the throne in A. D. 985. He maintained a large standing army of well-disciplined bodyguards, foot soldiers and archers, that was ever in readiness for active service, and with the aid of his valiant troops he quelled the rebellion of Kandalur Salai, subdued the Vengi and Ganga countries, defeated and humbled the Chalukyas, deprived the Pandyas of their splendour, took Ceylon and thus distinguished himself; we read in one of his inscriptions, that he was worthy of worship everywhere. From 1001 A. D., he sheathed his sword and cultivated the arts of peace. When he ascended the throne, the Chola kingdom hardly comprised the districts of Trichinopoly and Tanjore and a portion of the district of Coimbatore. Before he died, he had destroyed the Chera fleet, his power extended over the whole of the modern Presidency of Madras, part of Mysore, the island of Ceylon, Burma, the Laccadives and the

Maldives. It was he who built the Brihatîswara Temple at Tanjore, one of the grandest specimens of Dravidian architecture in Southern India.

Though a great Saiva devotee he seems to have been tolerant of other sects and creeds. A set of twenty-one copper plates, preserved now in the University museum of Leyden in Holland, hence known as the Leyden Grant, records the interesting fact that he granted a village to a Buddhist vihara at Negapatam, a monastery which was probably on the site of the present St. Joseph's buildings in that town.

The regulations for the levy of taxes and the minuteness with which the land measurements were made indicate the great care bestowed by Raja Raja in the administration of the large empire which he had built up during his reign. From 1011 A. D. his son Rajendra ruled the country along with the father as heir-apparent.

Throughout the Madras Presidency, we meet with his *copper kasu* in large numbers. Every itinerant pedlar who barters pepper, turmeric and spices for old copper is able to get together, after a week's labour, a large number of these specimens current more than nine hundred years ago. The commonest of these bear on their obverse a standing human figure clad in regal robes, and on the reverse the same figure seated, with the legend in Devanagiri characters, 'Raja Raja,' under the right arm. Coins with similar devices and legend occur also but more rarely in silver and gold.

The Chola emblem generally found on seals, is a seated tiger; on the coins of the later Chola sovereigns the figure of the seated tiger is found flanked by the fish, the Pandyan emblem, and the bow, the Chera emblem. Yet this characteristic Chola device of the tiger is not generally to be found on the coins of Raja Raja. The only known instance in which the dynastic device is figured on his issues is a coin in impure silver, on the obverse of which is the typical squatting human figure above referred to with a seated tiger flanked by lamps and surmounted by a parasol, with on the reverse the seated tiger, the fish and the bow, the Chola, Pandya and Chera emblems respectively. On the other hand, the standing and seated human figures adverted to already are familiar symbols of the Sinhalese sovereigns of Ceylon nearly two centuries later. Raja Raja's coins are usually referred to as those of the Ceylon type. The adoption of this so-called Ceylon type by Raja Raja, the greatest monarch of his age, must be of real significance. "The history of Ceylon from very early times down to the fourteenth century is the history of the struggles of the Aryan islanders to hold their own against the ever-increasing numbers of the Dravidian hordes. Twelve times the Tamils became masters of the plains and twelve times the Sinhalese issued forth from their mountain strongholds to drive their enemies back across the sea." We have come across no indigenous Sinhalese coinage prior to the time of Parakramabahu who began to rule in the middle of the 12th Century. We are thus not in a position to know what exactly the indigenous type of coinage in Ceylon was. In excavations in Ceylon carried out by Mr. Bell were discovered rectangular coins such as are found in the Madura and Tinnevelly Districts. There is nothing in them to indicate that the rudely executed standing and seated figures first appearing on the coins of Raja Raja had been the symbol or badge of the Sinhalese kings. To say therefore that the coins of Raja Raja, the mightiest conqueror of his time, were of the Ceylon type or Ceylon-man type is to make many groundless assumptions. If the gold *madais* of Raja Raja are found in Ceylon it is because Raja Raja had conquered Ceylon and established his supremacy over the island.

Coins too are not uncommon on which the legend 'Raja Raja' appears along with the Pandyan emblem, the fish, and the Chalukyan emblem, the boar. Specimens with a seated figure and the Devanagari legend, 'Raja Raja' have on the reverse also the legend 'Sekhara' written twice. Two gold *madais* with the legends, Lankesvara and Raja Raja were probably issued by Raja Raja in Ceylon after his conquest of the Island. On the obverse of these coins appears the figure intended to represent a king in regal robes, with other emblems familiarly seen on the copper cash of Raja Raja and on the reverse, the same figure seated, with the legend Raja Raja Lankesvara, in Devanagari.

Others there are attributable to this Chola king, which bear distinctly Vaishnavite emblems such as the Vishnupada or feet of Vishnu, or the figure of Krishna as Muralidhara (the flute player), familiar objects of worship among the Vaishnavas. This fact is another instance of the king's religious toleration which made him endow a Buddhist monastery, and a Siva temple at about the same time.

In still other specimens bearing the legend, Raja Raja, there is on the obverse the representation of a galloping horseman; but the significance of this symbol it is not yet possible to definitely determine.

Rajendra succeeded his father Raja Raja in 1011 A.D. and vanquishing the Ganga prince after a sanguinary war assumed the surname of Gangai Konda Chola. Like his father he was ceaseless in activity in humbling his rivals and annexing their dominions and making the Chola rule steadfast from Kalinga in the north to Kumari in the south. He it was, who probably built the temple and settled in the place called after him, Gangaikonda Cholapuram, in the Udaiyarpalayam Taluk of the Trichinopoly District. Like his father he took delight in parading in his inscriptions what was very likely a fact that he had humbled the Pandyas and Cheras. During his reign another intermarriage with the Chalukyas of Vengi served to further cement the relationship first brought about by the marriage of Raja Raja's daughter to a Chalukya prince.

The coins of Gangai Konda Chola have the same devices both on the obverse and the reverse. 'In the centre is a seated tiger, the emblem of the Chola king facing the right with two fishes, the emblem of the Pandyan king in front, and a bow, the emblem of the Chera king, behind, the whole group flanked by two lamps and surmounted by a parasol and two chowries.' Underneath is the legend in Devanagari characters, 'Gangaikonda Chola' in two lines. Two other silver coins are also known. one bearing the legend 'Sri Rajendra' and the other the legend 'Uttama Chola' in Devanagari characters both of the same type as the coins bearing the legend 'Gangaikonda Chola' already noticed. The first of these was evidently issued before the conquest of the Ganga country by Parakesari Varman, *alias* Rajendra Deva and the latter seems to have been issued when he assumed the surname Uttama Chola. As already pointed out the title *Uttama Chola* had also been assumed by Madurantaka son of Gandaraditya, and the predecessor of Raja Raja.

In the first half of the eleventh century five kings ruled between the time of Gangaikonda Chola and that of Kulottunga Chola who ascended the throne in A.D. 1070. They all recount in their inscriptions in high sounding terms their warlike exploits and conquests over the neighbouring kingdoms. But there is a blank in the coinage of this period and no coins of these five sovereigns have hitherto been discovered.

In 1071 A.D. the daughter's son of Rajendra Chola, who was ruling from 1061 in Vengi or the Chalukya country succeeded also to the Chola throne. He assumed the name, Kulottunga Chola, and ruled over the southern country for nearly half a century. He had been adopted by Rajendra *alias* Gangaikonda Chola as heir-apparent to the throne, but only succeeded in obtaining the sovereignty by force in the year 1070 A.D. some nine years after he had become ruler of Vengi. The province of Vengi was thereafter entrusted by him to his uncle first, and then to his sons, one of whom Vira Chola assumed the office of Viceroy in 1078 A. D.

Kulottunga I conquered the Kerala, Pandya and Kuntala countries and was anointed in the Chola kingdom as Kulottunga Chola Deva. It is not possible without encroaching much on the reader's time, to recount the doings of Kulottunga during a long reign. He ruled from both Gangaikonda Cholapuram and Kanchipuram; the latter place which was only second in importance became a Chola city after the subversion of the Pallavas in the eigth century A. D.

One would expect that such a long reign could be illustrated by a fairly large variety of coins but the results of numismatic research till now have been disappointing. Some years ago there was a find of sixteen gold coins in the Krishna District, which are now in the Government Central Museum at Madras. The coin bears the following emblems:—'Centre: A boar facing the proper left and surrounded by two lamps, an elephant goad, a parasol, and two indistinct emblems' Margin, Sri Raja Raja Samvat-34. The coins bear the legend on the obverse, while the *punchmarks* show through on the plain reverse. The irregular concave shape of the obverse was evidently caused by the gradual bending of the coin during the application of six several punches to make the impressions on the coins.'

In the same series have to be placed other coins which show on the 'obverse a boar and on the reverse the legend 'Chola Narayana.' The first of these is surmised to be that of Kulottunga's father, the Eastern Chalukyan king, Raja Raja, who ruled between A.D. 1022-1063; while the latter is attributed to Kulottunga himself from the fact that he had borne the surname, Rajanaryana. I have already referred to the copper pieces having on the obverse the standing figure, as in Raja Raja's coins, and on the reverse, a standing boar with a Telugu or Canarese legend above, which may be read Prapa. But unless better specimens are procured and further research throws more light on the coinage of this period nothing definite can be stated about the reign in which the coin was issued.

The Chola power after Kulottunga I began gradually to wane and the last king with any pretensions to power was Kulottunga III, 1278 A.D. By the year 1234 A.D. we see a Hoysala king established in the Chola country with his capital at Kannanore near Samayapuram. We hear also that Raja Raja III was captured by a Perum Singa and had to be rescued by a Hoysala king who consequently prided himself by assuming the title of the 'Establisher of the Chola Kingdom.' At this time too, the Pandyan power which had so long been subject to the Cholas, received a fresh impetus under Mara Varman Sundra Pandya who boasts of having burnt Tanjore and Uraiyur, presented the Chola kingdom to a favourite, but when the Chola prostrated at his feet made a free gift of the kingdom to him. Thus we find in the end of the thirteenth century, the Cholas decline and fall, after having for nearly four centuries been the sole arbiters of the destinies of Dravida Desam.

The coins belonging to this period of Chola sovereignty have not yet been found; but there are with me unassigned coins which possibly refer to the successors of Kulottunga. On the obverse of all these is the standing figure so often referred to above, while on the reverse is the figure of a standing bull, with the Devanagari syllable vi, which may stand for Vira Chola, or the Canarese syllable '*vi*,' which may stand for 'Vikarama Chola', the immediate successor of Kulottunga *alias* Rajendra. It may not be improbable too that to more than one Raja Raja that ruled after Kulottuuga we have to attribute the more modern looking of the copper issues bearing the legend, Raja Raja.

Some of the Pandyan coins of this period throw light on the low ebb to which the Chola power had been reduced by various causes. One coin bears the legend 'Kachi Valangum Perumal' which means that a Pandyan king after taking the Chola town, Kanchipuram, in battle, gave it back generously to the vanquished Chola prince. The other records that the Pandyan king conquered the Chola country, in the brief legend "Chonadu Kondan." This briefly is the story of the Chola coinge as far as it is known at present. By far the commonest of them are the copper cash of Raja Raja; the gold and silver pieces are rare. The issues of a large number of the Chola sovereigns have yet to be deciphered. Vast quantities of these valuable store-houses of information are annually going 'to the goldsmith's crucible and the brazier's melting pot' and it is the duty of every earnest enquirer into the condition of Ancient India to rescue them from this cruel fate.

The Coins of Vijaiyanagar

In the fourteenth century, as every other indigenous kingdom was waning in importance, the now 'Forgotten Empire' grew into power. Just about the same time the Mughal viceroys who usurped sovereign power began also to rule in different parts of the Deccan and the Peninsula.

The coinage of the Forgotten Empire of Vijaiyanagar was in gold and copper and not in lead or silver. A few silver specimens attributed by ardent numismatists and enthusiastic antiquaries of the type of 'Monkbarns' to the reign of Deva Roya have been treasured in their cabinets. During the last quarter of a century not more than half a dozen of Devaroya silver fanams have filtered into the collections of these votaries of numismatics. But I entertain no doubt that these silver Devaroyas were in recent times begotten in Tirupati or some such other centre of manufacture of brass gods and things of that ilk by the adventure and enterprise of a silversmith who essayed to turn an honest Rupee by imitating, in silver, the gold fanams of Devaroya, so that when gilded they might go into a string of an antique-looking necklace, adored by the antiquary.

Ramatankas of Vijaiyanagara origin have become through various adventitious causes objects of worship in Indian households. Gold itself, by its superb colour, intrinsic value and other enchanting influences which still abide, has been an object of worship in Dravidam, if not elsewhere. And when, on coins or medals of a quaint cup-shaped form, the story of the national epic was imprinted on the obverse of these the coronation of Sri Rama and thus immortalised it in Swarna, no wonder the Ramatankas commanded reverence, grew into esteem and in due time even their imitations acquired a fictitious value. The religious instinct inseparable from Puranic Hinduism, was not neglected, for on the reverse of these revered medals was imprinted a double, square interlaced, with the prayer, in Canarese, '*Sri Iswarayanamah*' each syllable in one of the triangles formed by the superimposed squares the central space in the geometrical figure being assigned to so dear a figure to the religious enthusiast as that of 'Hanuman.' And none but the experienced numismatist could distinguish the real from the spurious 'Rama tankas' and 'Umamaheswari' Pagodas which pass for Indian antiquities.

A similar uncertainty hangs over the fate of the silver issues of Deva Roya and the owner of them may start as from a dream when, with regard to his dearly cherished possession, he has but to share the disappointment of Jonathan Oldbuck at what time he was disillusioned, about the claim of the Kaim of Kinprunes for being the local situation of the final conflict of Agricola and the Caledonians, by the unceremonious pronouncement of Edi Ochiltree. Such silver Devaroyas as I have knowledge of, and I believe they complete the tale thereof, seem to have their cradle in the land of fertile art and religion, the far-famed shrine of Venkateswara.

The emblems on the coins of Vijaiyanagara, which abound in large numbers and great variety, coming from almost every one of the kings of all the three lines, but demonstrate the old and true lesson that the Puranic religion had by the fourteenth century completely revived and become what regulated the faith of the most powerful indigenous kingdom of the South.

Harihara, Vira Bhupati, Vijaya Bukka, Mallikarjuna, Deva, Krishna, Achyuta, Rama and Sri Ranga are among the Royas whose reigns are represented by the coins which have found their way into well-known numismatic cabinets in South India.

The most numerous are the copper issues of Deva Roya bearing on their obverse the figure of a bull and on their reverse, amidst significant emblems the Canarese legend, Deva Roya. Some of his *birudas or* titles also occur on the issues of his reign such as 'Nilakanta,' 'Uttama', and 'Raya Gajaganda Bherunda' in Devanagari.

The coins of the earlier kings bear distinctly Saivite emblems like the seated Siva and Parvati while those of the later monarchs have decidedly Vaishnava devices, thus affording a striking proof of the religious evolution, studied nowhere better than in Chola Mandalam. It is not however unusual for the same sovereign to exhibit his religious or sectarian neutrality, by issuing coins bearing the emblems borrowed from both the Saiva and Vaishnava cults. The spirit of toleration which was the essential feature of the ancient Vedic faith, seems to have been fostered by the pupils of Vidyaranya and the earlier princes of the Vijaiyanagara line. Would that the same sane spirit ruled the adherents of the rival cults of the same faith to-day!

In the early series the legends are in Canarese generally, on the later, they are in Devanagiri. A similar change is perceptible in the Chola coinage: the Tamil Grandha in the earlier issues, giving place to the classical though less popular Devanagari in the later ones.

The following are some of the devices on Vijaiyanagara coins and to the student of symbols and symbolism they tell their own intelligent and intelligible tale:—"Siva and Parvati" on the gold pagodas of Harihara and Devaroya; the bull on the gold coins of Vijaiya Bukka Roya and Sri Devaroya; the figures of Vishnu and his two consorts on the issues of the later kings; the Ganda Bherunda—a mythical double-headed eagle holding elephants in its beaks and claws—and the boar, on the issues of Achyuta Roya; the figure of Hanuman on the coins of Bhupathi Roya; and the figure of Garuda on those of Pratapa Krishna Roya.

Tthe pagodas of Vijaiyanagar form the links between the Chalukya Padma Tankas and the 'star' and the 'three swami' pagodas of the English East India Company, the crescent pagoda of the French East India Company, the 'Tegnapatam' pagoda of the Dutch East India Company and the 'C_7' pagoda of the Danish East India Company. It is instructive to note the transmission to comparatively modern times of the persistent impress cast upon South Indian currency by the ancient Pœnician metrical and monetary standards, despite the ravages of time and the rise and fall of many powerful empires. And if the stupendous ruins of Hampi remind us of the greatness of the last great Hindu kingdom of the South, its prolific mint no less significantly demonstrates its wealth and importance, the share it had in making India what it is, moulding into an almost indestructable shape the manners, society, polity and religion of the South India down to the 20th century A.D.

The Coins of Ma'abar

The Muhammadan usurpers of the Mughal power did even in their doubtful political situation mint their symbols of sovereignty in the peninsula, Indian. These issues were in copper, billon and silver, in the earlier reigns and included gold in the latter. Of these some were published by Mr. Rogers and others by myself and Diwan Bahadur T. M. Rengachariar, Retired District Judge. The specimens brought together so far illustrate the history of the Bahmini kings of Deccan, the Adilshahai Dynasty of Bijapur, the Nizam Shahi Dynasty of Ahmadnagar and the Kutb Shahi Dynasty of Golconda.

A great number of issues bearing the legend Muhammed Bin Toglakh and many of his forced '*tankas*' are ordinarily met with in the modern districts of Tinnevelly, Ramnad, Madura and Trichinopoly as well as in the Districts north of Trichinopoly, though there somewhat less numerously. These 'ma'abar coins' unlike those of the Hindu sovereigns of the south belonging to the period of their currency bear the index of the place of their mintage and the year of their issue. This is the characteristic distinction between the coins of Muhammedan and Hindu origin. The usurper Tippu Sultan was as fastidious about the place of mintage and the date of his coins as the proudest Moghal in the palmy days of his supremacy. The distinction draws too attention and gives point to the cardinal difference between the two civilisations which have coalesced and are doing so in India, the one looking to such mundane concerns as have count on time and space and the other on the dreamy and ultramundane satisfaction attained in the propitiation of the names of deceased ancestors.

The coinage of the various petty principalities which each loomed great at some period or other of the eventful struggles for domination in India south of the Vyndhya mountains, has yet to be treated with accuracy and in details. Such an investigation is bound to lead us to a more just and definite understanding of the part which the adherents of the militant faith of Islam did undoubtedly play in giving us the large body of British Indian Moslems, converts to the faith of the Prophet by the sword or by more peaceful means, from the faith of Puranic Hinduism. The coins of the Nawabs of the Carnatic and the Muhammedan usurpers of Mysore have already received detailed treatment at the hands of numismatists. A comprehensive and rational study of South Indian Muhammedan coinage or, the Ma'abar coins, as I venture to call them, has yet to be attempted. And I am sure that when that is done the sum of historical knowledge in one of most interesting periods in South Indian history will receive a notable addition.

Notes on the Indo-Dutch Coinage

The Dutch who at one time were no mean rivals of the English East India Company and had exercised undisputed supremacy over the Eastern seas have curiously enough no settlements at the present day in India. In the seventeenth century they had established themselves in the island of Java, wrested the Moluccas and Ceylon from the earlier Portuguese settlers and owned many settlements on the Coromandel coast of the Indian mainland, the ruins of some of which situated a few miles from Madras still recall the old days of Dutch rule in India. But it is an old and well-worn tale, the fall of the Dutch, brought about by their greed and cruelty and their dream of a Dutch India was shattered once for all by Lord Clive when he took Chinsura, their capital in Bengal, in 1758.

It is not the monumental remains still to be found in the old Dutch settlements that alone remind one of the unsuccessful struggle of the Dutch for power in India. The issues of their prolific mint bear silent witness to the ambitions of a power which vied for supremacy in the East with the other great people from western Europe to whose care are happily committed the destinies of this land.

By far the most familiar of these coins are those artistically executed pieces known *Nagore challies*, bearing on the obverse the monogram "V. O. C." standing for "vereenigde Oost Indische compagnie," meaning "United East India Company." These form five series, each having a different coat of arms on the reverse according to the state represented :—

(a) The *Utrecht* series having a plain divided shield supported by a *lion rampant* on either side.

(b) The *Gelderland* series bearing within a divided shield *two lions combatant* with the legend around "*In Deo est spes nostra.*"

(c) The *Holland* series with the whole shield occupied by a *lion rampant* facing the left.

(d) The *Zeeland* series with a *demi-lion rampant* emerging out of the sea, with often the legend around "Luctor et emergo."

(e) The *Friesland* series bearing on their reverse two lions *passant gardant* within a plain divided shield.

These coins seem to have been issued during a period of eighty years from 1727 to 1806 A.D. and a large number of each series can be collected even now for each decade, in the old Dutch settlements in Southern India, though as far as I know no challies for certain years notably 1795 to 1800 could be secured. It will be interesting to discover whether any coins were minted in these years, and if so what accounts for their disappearance altogether, when challies even of later years are procurable in abundance. The obverse of the coins which, as above described, bears the monogram, made up of the letters O and C superscribed over the arms of the letter V, at first sight uniform, presents on closer inspection many distinctive features, due to the devices over the monogram, such as a flower, a cock, a plain shield, a castle or a galloping horse, all of which must have served as mint marks so common in those days. Nor does the variety stop here, for coins with legends like "*over yssel,*" "*Zeelandia*" and "*stad utrecht*" are also known.

Of half challies there are at least three varieties, the first from 1749 to 1753 with the Holland coat of arms; the second with a plain divided shield running upto 1759 and the third represented by coins of 1770 bearing the Freisland or Zeeland coat of arms. There seems to have been also a double challi comprised in this currency, but hitherto only one such coin has been, so far as we know found in S. India.

The Numismatic enthusiast also meets with a later variety of coins, on which the monogram of the Company ceases to figure on the obverse, bearing the legend "Nederland India" "Java" and "India Batav" all of which are multiples or fractions of the Dutch unit of mintage, the stuiver.

The coins hitherto dealt with were all primarily intended for circulation in the Dutch possessions other than their Indian settlements, and are all so carefully executed and well designed, that there can be little doubt of their having been coined in the mother country. Simultaneously with the issue of these coins from a European mint, others were struck locally, in most if not all of the Dutch settlements, comprising two, one, half and quarter stuiver pieces. These are thick lumps of copper, irregular in shape and ill designed, and in most of them the letters "S. T." standing for "stuiver" are reversed. Those issued for circulation in Ceylon, bear over the monogram of the Company, the letter "G" standing for "Galle" "C" for "Columbo,"

"இல" for "Ilangai" or Ceylon and "T" for "Trincomalle." The letter T however might with equal reason be taken to have represented the mint towns Tuticorin or Tegnapatam. In one coin is found under the date the Tamil Syllable "புவ" "Puva" whose significance is not known. The Dutch settlements on the Coromandel coast also possessed mints of their own. Those issued from Pulicat bore the Persian Legend Zerbe "Pulicat"—pice of Pulicat, in consonance with the fashion, of the European East India Companies of the time, of imprinting Persian legends on their coins either to secure them a uniformity with the indigenous currency of the land or more probably to cater to the taste of their trading customers. The reverse of these coins bore the company's monogram with the letter "P," or in the coins of the higher denominations the letters "Pal," standing for "Palliacat." The Dutch coins from Negapatam had the letter "N" over the monogram on one side and the Tamil legend நாகப்பட்டணம் on the reverse. From the very commencement of their trade in the East, the Dutch issued coins in silver, as will be evident from specimens bearing the legend 'Frisia' 'Transilvania,' 'Zeelandia' and "India Batavorum" the prettiest of the lot being a six stuiver piece with the representation on the obverse of a ship in full sail. Silver stuvier pieces, equal to twenty or forty cash appear to have been issued by the Company but all traces of these coins have been lost in South India. Like the other trading companies, however, the Dutch also seem to have coined money in *lead* or *tutenag*. The Andhra Kingdom, in the early centuries of the Christian Era, is known to have possessed a lead coinage and in more recent times both the Portuguese and the English East India Companies had their money both in lead and copper, the latter Company having issued lead coins, known as *budgrooks* (Port: Bazarucco) for currency in the settlement of Bombay in the reigns of Charles II and the first three Georges. It is noteworthy that no Dutch coins in lead have hitherto come to light.

The Dutch coined money also in gold, the Dutch pagoda being very similar in size to the French, Danish and English pagodas of the period. The obverse bore the effigy of Vishnu (one of the Hindu Trinity) surrounded by the legend Tevenapatam (Tegnapatam having been one of the Dutch settlement in India). The gold currency of the European traders in the East approximated very much to that of the last great Hindu kingdom of Vijayanagar and the Dutch not improbably adopted the effigy of Vishnu in imitation of the English East India Company who were bound by treaty to issue pagodas with such a figure on their obverse. But the weight of the pagoda seems to have been made to agree with that of the European ducats already introduced into India and familiar already as a medium of currency between the foreign merchants and the natives of the land. The company's gold and silver *fanams*, of which a pretty large number must have been issued, are not at all to be met with. Their value is supposed to have equalled four stuivers.

This brief survey of the coinage of the Dutch East India Company cannot be closed without reference being made to a practice prevailing in their settlements of impressing with a seal, the monogram of the Company, V. O. C., on any foreign coin that was received by them. Broad silver pieces of Tiflis have been discovered in which the monogram of the Company have been imprinted thus rendering them current in the Dutch settlement in which they were received. The practice of "punchmarking" was not new to India and among the indigenous coins, those current at one time were adopted as the currency of a later period by being "punched" with seals bearing appropriate emblems. A similar device seems to have been adopted in recent times in the converion of dollars into Double Arcot Rupees.

Only the leading types of the coinage of the Dutch East India Company that might filter into the hands of the coin hunter in South India have been dealt with above, but the reader who is inclined to take up the fascinating subject of South Indian numismatics will be astonished at the many varieties of coins issued by a trading Company with possessions in the East so limited as those of the Dutch in the latter half of the 18th century.

Indo-French Coins

The history of the rise and fall of the French Power in India, the heroic endeavours of more than one illustrious French General for the attainment of universal dominion in the East Indies, and the brilliant achievements of the Great Frenchman, who, though unsupported at home and badly served here, by his mighty genius and indomitable energy, caused the fame of the French nation to redound in the palaces of Delhi and the armies of the subordinate sovereignties in the Carnatic, are all familiar to the student of Indian History.

The French were the last of the great maritime powers to direct their attention to the benefits resulting from a trade with the East. But their great genius and restless ambition made them outstrip their rivals and conceive plans for the establishment of a European Empire in the East, plans which on the very brink of success failed, and being followed out by another great European power, led to the rise and progress of an Empire to which all of us do at present owe our allegiance.

I do not here propose to recount the interesting doings of the French in India during the momentous era preceding the total annihilation of their great hopes but have set myself a humbler task, viz. that of giving a brief account of their coinage in Pondichery and the other French settlements in the East.

Following the example of the rival European powers who had established commercial communication and intercourse with India, on 24th June 1642 the French also organised an India Company on the model of the earlier Dutch East India Company. This Company however went into abeyance after a brief period of very promising activity.

This was succeeded in 1664 by an Association, under the title and designation of "The East India Company" with a fifty years' monopoly to trade with all the Colonies of the Indian Ocean, from the East coast of Africa to the Sunda Islands.

It became amalgamated in 1720 with "The West India Company" under the title of "The Perpetual Company of the Indies".

The Constitution was changed from time to time, till, in 1791, by a decree of the Constitutional Assembly freedom of trade was proclaimed to all. The currency I shall treat of, originally introduced for meeting the exigencies and local needs of the factories of these trading corporations, gradually assumed the importance of an emblem of regal power and the exercise of a Sovereign privilege.

In all countries and especially in India, the coining of money was ever considered as the right and emblem of Sovereignty. The European companies who first established factories in India were impelled by the force of circumstances to gradually acquire territory and administer it. They soon realised, that to be treated and respected as governors of the territory possessed by them, it was essential that they should exercise the privilege of maintaining a currency of their own. Thus the British East India Company when obtaining the modern Madras from the Rajah of Chandraghiri had an article inserted in their grant, conceding to them the right to coin their own money. But these trading corporations who set up as petty sovereigns were in an anomalous position; while they continued to be the subjects of their sovereign, they had to acknowledge the supremacy of the Potentate or Chief within whose jurisdiction lay their territory. Their coinage too thus came to occupy a similar anomalous position. Issued by a Christian power, the coins bore effigies of Hindu Gods or the legends and devices peculiar to the Mahomedan rule and religion; thus giving rise to a fruitful theme for controversy between those who were responsible for the material welfare of the territories acquired and those entrusted with the administration of their spiritual affairs. Moreover, the state of the Carnatic in the period immediately preceding the advent of European merchants to India was such as to necessiate the exercise of a privilege, deemd to be the valued right and the chief symbol of sovereign power. Owing to the fall of the last great Hindu Kingdom of Vijianagar the country was split up into many small principalities, each practically independent, though in some cases acknowledging the paramountcy of the Emperor of Delhi; each warring against another and courting the assistance of marauding hordes or foreign merchants who exercised sovereign power, in carrying on their devastating internecine wars. The French East India Company therefore early recognised the value of having their own mint, and the papers relaing to the acquisition by them of this much coveted and valued privilege are very interesting reading, and I shall quote here the translation of some of them, kindly made for me by the Rev. Father Newton of the St. Joseph's College, Trichinopoly, from M. Zay's History of the French coinage in India.

To understand these papers it is first necessary to know exactly what the monetary system prevailing in India was, in the troublous times under reference, which system the French India Company was pledged to adopt and follow. Money was coined in gold, silver, copper and lead; the gold *pagoda*, the silver *fanam* and the *kash* in copper or lead. To these were added coins in *tutenag* and rupees in silver. The *fanam* and *kash* are indigenous terms and the old *Kahapana* or *Karsha*, is met with as the designations of coins even during the time preceding the Christian Era. But the origin of the word *pagoda* is obscure and the name itself is unknown in the ancient monetary system of India. The indigenous "*Swarna*" or gold coin could alone have been familiar to the Mahomedan rulers or European merchants in their early commercial intercourse in India as the unit of gold currency, which had taken a firm hold in the land. The ancient name of these gold coins was the Sanskrit "*Swarna*" or the Tamil "*Pon*" or the Hindustani "*Hun.*" Owing to the adoption of the device of the "*Varaha avatara*" of Vishnu, on these coins, in the period of Chalukya ascendency in the South of India, in the 6th and 7th Centuries of the Christian Era, the *Swarna* came to be known as "*varaha.*" On gold coins of the weight, fineness and shape of these *Swarnas* the kings of the last Great Hindu Empire imprinted in the 14th and 15th centuries various figures from the Hindu Pantheon, principally those of Vishnu and Siva, with or without their consorts. These *huns* probably then began to be known as "*Bagavathis*" and "*Baghavatas*", corrupted terms signifying the figures of the Goddess or God which appeared on these coins. The temples in which these idols were worshipped were probably known as "*Buth Goda*" or temple of God. Thus the coins themselves came to be named "*Baghavadas*" or "*Buthgodas*" by the Portuguese merchants, who, but imperfectly understanding the significance of the terms, by a natural mental confusion, applied to the coins themselves the generic names they gave to the figures found on them. Whatever the real origin of the nomenclature then current, the fact is that the 'pagoda' was in the 15th and 16th centuries the acknowledged unit of gold currency in South India and no commercial transaction could be carried on without the *Pagoda.*

So jealous were the Indian princes in preserving the uniformity and the characteristic feature of their currency that they seem to have insisted, when granting to any one the privilege of coining money, on the effigy of a Hindu God or Goddess appearing on the coins issued from the mint of the grantee. This was one of the conditions in the Chandragiri grant in favour of the English East India Company already referred to, so that their *Pagodas* invariably had the figure of Vishnu or of Vishnu and his two consorts on their coins.

The French East India Company likewise, when they issued their '*pagodas*', had to conform to the prevailing usage and submit to the necessities of the existing situation. I shall leave them to relate their position in their own language:—

PAGODAS

In the year 1705 the Chevalier Martin wishing to utilize the golden coins found in the cargo of the Phœnix d'or, a Dutch ship of 54 guns and 220 men captured in the fight of the 13 January, 1705 by post-captain Baron de Pallie'res, resolved to turn them into pagodas. That they might be received by the natives and so secure the currency denied to the French fanams, which, on account of their French type, were in circulation only in Pondichery and its territory, he adopted for these pagodas the type of the pagodas then current in the country and all along the Coromandel coast, under the name of *Varaha* (boar) or *Varaha moudra* (stamp of the boar). About 100,000 of them were coined. But the clergy of Pondichery and their head, the Bishop of Mylapore, remonstrated against the new issue, as the work though entrusted to Malabari workmen, had however been done for the sake of safety within the walls of Fort Louis in which the mint was situated.

In the issue of the pagoda with a Hindu device they pretended to see an act of homage to the deity thereon represented called by the Hindus, Lakshmi, the goddess of riches and plenty, "and that is the reason why in all important contracts they make it touch their mouth, eyes and forehead as a token of gratitude for the bargain concluded through her help, and of the hope that by this means the bargain will be profitable to them."

In consequence of the opposition of the Clergy the issue of *pagodas* was stopped; and the Supreme Council of Pondichery referred the matter to the Directors-General in Paris. "The Company," so runs the reply, "do not doubt that it is extremely advantageous to coin at their mint *pagodas* of the current standard; wherefore they order you to coin them wherever, and as often as, there will be an occasion and the service of the Company will require it."

"They consider the objections which the Church has against the mintage of this type of coin on account of the impression thereon of an idol, to be unfounded; the more so as no worship is paid to the coin and in all religions it is enjoined to render unto Cæsar that which is Cæsar's. Wherefore do not hesitate in the least to execute the Company's orders and should any opposition be made by the Clergy, continue all the same and refer them to the orders of the Company in Paris". To this injunction the Council replied, "We have set to work as regards the execution of your last orders, the contents of which we have shown to the persons hitherto opposed to it; they had nothing to say. And so the execution of the Company's orders will go on as usual."

In 1720 fresh protests elicited, a fresh rejoinder from the Directors: "It is certain," so they write to the Council, "that if you could get permission from the Moghul to coin in Pondichery gold *pagodas* of the same type and standard as his own, all difficulty would be at an end with the Rev. Fathers, Jesuits, Capuchins and Missionaries, since the Moghul coins bear only Arab characters; but if, on the other hand, minting such coins is forbidden to Europeans and they are allowed to mint only such as bear the device of the *pagoda*, why should we not have the same advantages as the English who in Madras mint these latter,[1] thereby making an assured profit for themselves? Do the missionaries refuse to take these coins from individuals who owe them to them? Do they say that they do not want them because they bear the figure of an idol? No: they are wiser than that, they make good use of them. There is no more harm in coining such pagodas than in using them; continue then to issue them since they are required not only for daily use, but also for commerce." While acknowledging receipt of this notification the Council observes that "the Moghul's permission is not needed for minting these coins which have currency only on this coast (Coromandel)".

CORRESPONDENCE

between the Supreme Council of Pondichery and the Bishop of San Thome on the subject of the coinage of pagodas.

Translation of a letter written by the members of the Supreme Council to his Lordship, the Bishop of St. Thome.

13th May, 1705.

My Lord, the situation in which we find ourselves since the departure home of our ships, having obliged us to turn into coins of the country the gold we had in our stores in order that we might face the expenses we daily incur as well in promoting the Company's

---

[1] Pagoda with a star at the back.

commerce and constructing our fort, as in paying and maintaining our garrison, the Rev. Jesuit and Capuchin Fathers of this town have reprehended us for having placed the ordinary stamp of the country, viz., a *pagoda*, on the money we coined. As we have been forced to do as we did in our present state of affairs, and as far from having any intention of promoting the worship of idols as we are reproached with doing, we have only had in view to procure the good and profit of our Company by a means which seemed to us without harm to religion, we take the liberty to address your Lordship as our Pastor and our Bishop in order to disclose the motives that have determined us in this affair and to receive at your hands the means of restoring calm to our consciences, which they (the Fathers) are trying to make a prey to terrible scruples.

After the departure of our ships, the few pagodas left us having been disposed of, we tried to acquire more by selling the gold we had in store. The merchants of this country who knew our great need, and who saw besides that we were about to begin our fourth bastion—which meant a considerable increase of expenses in the future—kept tight and made no offers or only at so unreasonable a price that we could not accept but at considerable loss to the Company. However, time was passing, and our monthly expenses amounting to a large number of *pagodas*, we found ourselves for a whole fortnight without a single *pagoda* in our office and on the point of being forced to stop the fortifications, and the Company's commerce and the soldiers' pay. This peril added to the sickness of the Chevalier Martin who was in danger of death, made us fear, and with reason, for the honour of the Company, should we in the event of his death come to the extreme plight mentioned above. These reasons then decided us to coin the gold we had in hand. The next point was to decide what stamp the money should bear; at last after consulting the merchants, as our needs were increasing from day to day and it was indispensable to us to have money with ready currency, and as everybody assured us that our coins would be useless unless they bore the stamp commonly used in this country, we have been compelled to stamp them with a *pagoda*, like the other coins current on this coast. Such are, my lord, the motives which have impelled us to have recourse to this measure; we repeat that we have the honour to address your Lordship in order that your charity may inspire you to instruct us should we have gone wrong.

Translation of the answer made to the above letter by the Lord Bishop of St. Thome, dated 4th June, 1705.

Gentlemen, I have read your letter and the motives you have had for minting *pagodas* with the stamp which the Gentiles use according to their custom. I am convinced of your Christian probity as of that of all French gentlemen, and of your having taken this step not with the intention of showing any honour to the idol but only to supply the need you had of that money. I know, moreover, the zeal you have for the destruction of the temples of Gentiles and of their religion; however, since the Gentiles stamp their coins with the figure of their idol to do it honour, it might seem as if Catholics, by minting such coins, were willing to participate in the intention of the Gentiles, an intention, however, which it would be too rash to impute to you; but, for this very reason, I cannot approve that you should stamp pagodas with the figure of the idol, the more so when I reflect that the most Christian King might be displeased that you should stamp money with the figure of the idol instead of with his arms. The quality and weight of the gold being the same as that of the current pagodas, the latter will be generally received by all, just as the "St. Thome" with the figure of the St. Thomas and the arms of Portugal are received throughout India. You have stamped *fanams* with the royal arms of France; you might similarly coin pagodas with a fleur-de-lis on one side and a chogron[1] or anything else on the other. This is what I believe should be my answer to your letter. I shall be ever ready to render you my humblest services.

Translation of a letter of the Chevalier Martin written to the Lord Bishop of St. Thome, 15th June, 1705.

My Lord, I have had the honour to address your Lordship through the Sieurs de Flacourt and de Hardancourt concerning the *pagodas* which necessity obliged us to have coined in Pondichery. I have received the answer that your Lordship has been pleased to send us dated the 4th of this month. We have had inquiries made as to the possibility of using the expedient proposed by your Lordship, *viz*, to give the *pagodas* the same device as our *fanams*; but notwithstanding the serious application given to the question we have been informed from the best sources that our

[1] In Sanskrit Tchakuram, a disc, one of the attributes of Vishnu.

pagodas would have no currency should they bear any other stamp than the ordinary one. True our *fanams* have currency, but only in Pondichery, while it is of the greatest importance to us that our *pagodas* should have currency throughout the country. The embarrassing position we are in, as your Lordship in answering has not absolutely condemned the said pagodas, has impelled us to apply to the Rev. Fr. Esprit our parish-priest and to the Rev. Frs. of the Society of Jesus to know their opinion on the subject; but this they absolutely refused to give. Therefore, My Lord, as the motives detailed in the previous letter continue to be valid and as we can find no other expedient to avoid stamping the pagodas according to the custom of the country, I beg your Lordship to be so good as to inform us whether we can in all safety of conscience continue to stamp the said pagodas; this affair is of the greatest consequence for the service of the Company.

Translation of the letter written by the Lord Bishop of St. Thome to the Chevalier Martin, 20 June, 1705 in answer to the above letter.

I thought I had answered the letter of the members of the Council with such clearness that there could remain no doubt as to the unlawfulness of coining pagodas with the figure of the idol. In fact, I said I could not approve of what the gentlemen had done; for, since the Gentiles stamped their coins with the figure of the idol to honour and worship it, it would look like co-operating with them in the worship they paid it............(I said)[1] I could not approve of it—an

[1] In the French text some words have been omitted, but the meaning is evidently as given above.

expression I used as being the most polite and respectful. It is certain that I disapproved of it, being incapable of giving my consent for a work of the kind to Roman Catholics and to such Catholics as Frenchmen, the evil being all the greater from these coins bearing the mark of Pondichery, a territory belonging to the French. It is certain too that His Most Christain Majesty will not approve of pagodas with the figure of an idol instead of his arms.

As to the fact that the *pagoda* stamped with the same device as the *fanams* would not have currency but in Pondichery, this does not prove that *pagodas* stamped with any other than an Indian device would have no currency—as in fact many of the Madras pagodas which are without the figure of the idol and some specimens of which I have in my possession, yet circulate throughout the country; and the Royal Company would derive the same profit from them as from the ones stamped with the figure of the idol. This is all I can say; wishing that you may improve in health so that I may rejoice when I receive your letters. God keep you etc., your very humble servant and friend.

BISHOP OF MILAPOR.

For copy of which the original documents are in the possession of the undersigned, Council Secretary to the Supreme and of the Royal Company of France,

DE LA PREVOSTIERE.

Pondichery, 30th Sept., 1705.

The *pagodas* eventually issued by the Company which so much irritated the religious susceptibilities of the Bishop of Mylapore bore on the obverse the figure of Vishnu and on the reverse on a granulated surface a crescent (an essentially Mahomedan device in deference to the wishes of the Mahomedan States of that period.) This coin was of the same value as that of the star *pagoda* of the English Company, the Dutch pagoda bearing the legend Tagnapatam and the Danish pagoda of Christian VII. This crescent *pagoda* ceased however to be minted long before the Revolution, the Pondichery mint having issued there after only *three Swami Pagodas* for the use of the settlement of Yanaon, similar to Madras Pagodas, with the figures of Vishnu and his consorts, on the obverse and the crescent on the reverse. A gold coin of a purely French type with a fleur-de-lis on the obverse is mentioned in certain lists but I have not come across any such specimen during the last twenty years.

Coming to the silver money, fanams began to be issued in the year 1700 and twenty six of these went to a gold pagoda. We are struck with the crude design and the imperfect execution of the issues of the European mints in India of the period, particularly when we remember that in the 15th and 16th centuries the currency of European countries had long emerged from their primitive stage and were not much inferior to the coins of Imperial Rome in exquisiteness of design and execution. But so inveterate was the influence of custom and prejudice in India that the European powers despite the facilities they had for issuing coins of an advanced type contented themselves with following the example of the people amidst whom they lived, and in some cases issued coins more rudely executed than those prevailing already in the country. Indeed the methods adopted for converting silver bars into coins with the aid of goldsmiths and Brahmin overseers were so rude and rudimentary that it is a wonder how by such primitive means, the currency of the French acquired its acknowledged importance and reputation in India. These *fanams* were originally made as nearly as possible of the standard then prevalent in the country. But the value of the currency having increased they were soon taken out of the country as there was profit in exporting them.

The Company thereupon devised a system whereby *fanams* of less weight, but still twenty-six to the *pagoda*, were issued, though really thirty-two of these were equivalent to the *pagoda*.

This had the effect of keeping the fanams within Pondichery and its territory, while by the withdrawal of the *fanams* from circulation by causes just like those operating in the present day, in the conversion of rupees into jewels and vessels, a large profit in gold resulted to the Company.

The designs on the coins however continued unaltered till the beginning of the 19th century except for the only change introduced by the substitution of the arms of the new Company for those of the old Company.

Three denominations of *fanams* were issued, 'the *fanan*', 'the double *fanan*', and 'the half *fanan*". The *earliest single fanan* bore on the obverse, within a circle, the legend "Pondichery 1700"; in the centre a fleur-de-lis and the reverse within a dotted rim four double Ls forming a cross and joined together by a circle with a fleur-de-lis in the centre. The *double fanan* had on the obverse a dotted rim within a dotted circle: a fleur-de-lis beneath a crown ornamented with fleur-de-lis. On the reverse, within a dotted rim were four double Ls forming a cross joined together by a circle within which was a fleur-de-lis. These types are essentially French, for there appears to have been no restriction imposed on the type of the silver and copper coinage of the country, they having taken only the place of cowries which passed as currency till very recent times. The Moghul Rupee alone of the silver coins of the period was sedulously guarded from being counterfeited and the efforts of the Company to secure the concession of coining Rupees will be dealt with presently. The two types of *fanams* above referred to were evidently issued by the first Company and are mentioned by M. Zay in his catalogue. But I have not come across these in the course of my coin hunting extending over nearly a quarter century. The coins issued by the second Company down to the year 1837 bear no distinctive marks to indicate the years in which they were issued. They comprise single and double *fanams* bearing on the obverse a small crown ornamented by a floral design and on the reverse five fleur-de-lis. These are ordinarily met with along with the *Puduchery* or "*Kolikas*" in the bazaars of almost all the Southern Districts. The archives of the Pondichery mint having been destroyed and the dies having disappeared, it is impossible to assign these fanams to any particular period. The typo of fanams of the third period is that bearing on the obverse the Gallic cock with the right claw on a globe, and date; and on the reverse a crown ornamented as in the last type of coins.

The copper coins of the Company which were of subordinate importance consisted of three types; the commonest are, (1) those with the legend Puducheri in Tamil on the reverse, and a large fleur de lis on the obverse, (2) the Gallic cock on the obverse with date 1836 or 1837 and a reverse which is the same as that of the first type. Along with these are often met with the coins issued during the Dutch occupation of Pondichery, (1) with the Tamil legends *Negapatam* on the obverse and the *Puducheri* on the reverse, (2) the Tamil legends, *Karaikal* on the obverse and *Nagapatam* on the reverse.

The French rupee, by coining which the Company made enormous profits, and which in course of time was greatly in request as of the finest silver obtainable in India during those times, was after the model of the Arcot rupee. The French had to wait a long time before obtaining the concession of issuing their own rupees. For nearly twenty-eight years from the year 1718, negotiations were going on with the Moghul Court at Delhi for securing the privilege of coining rupees, which formed the prevailing silver currency of the Moghul Empire. The French Company viewed with concern that their English rivals who enjoyed this privilege had thereby secured large profits and set about devising various means to cajole the Court of the Moghul into granting them the much desired concession. There was a certain St. Hilaire, at the Court of Delhi employed as the physician of the Great Mughul and the good offices of this Doctor were pressed into the aid of the diplomatic enterprises of the Company. A sum of Rs. 12,000 was offered through a Brahmin Ambassador as the price of the concession, but the Nawab who saw through the situation insisted on getting Rs. 25,000 brought by a Frenchman, who should also be the bearer of costly presents. The Company could not in their then financial condition undergo so great an expense for securing the privilege.

Then in 1724, M. Dupleix, nothing daunted by the failure of previous negotiations, worked again through the same St. Hilaire to secure the privilege of coining rupees, but despite the diplomatic skill of both these accomplished Frenchmen these fresh attempts proved also abortive.

In 1727, the loss resulting from the want of this privilege was very great, so much so that it prevented the sojourn in Pondichery of merchants from different parts of India; and when this was brought to the notice of the Directors of the Company at home they called for a fresh deliberation and decision of the Superior Council of Pondichery. The Council resolved to deal directly and at once with the Moghul, enjoining great secrecy in the preliminary negotiations; but nothing came out of these tactics either. Not till 1736 in the time of Governor Dumas was the long-wished-for announcement made in the following terms:—

"I have just been fortunate enough to do the Company a great service by obtaining from our Nawab permission in perpetuity to coin Rupees in Pondichery. This is no doubt one of the greatest and most honored privileges the French Nation has ever obtained in

India." The Company was enabled to obtain by the exercise of this privilege an annual profit of more than a lakh of Rupees.

The characteristic pomp and circumstance attending the confirmation of the Grant by the great Moghul, are indicated by the belated issue of three *parvanas*, a yadast from the Nawab of Bengal, another for Yanaon, and a third for Masulipatam. These were accompanied by a velvet and silk costume (serpo) as a mark of distinction.

It is interesting to note the price paid for securing the privilege which is duly recorded in the Diary of Dubash Ananda Ranga Pillai.

80,000 to the Nawab.

25,000 to his Court.

15,000 to Imam Saheb, the Treasurer of the Provinces, besides a family pension of Rs. 1000 per annum in Pondichery to the last-mentioned officer and about 8000 pagodas in various expenses and negotiations, which I suppose were not of such a character as could be set down in writing.

The Pondichery mint at one time coined so many as Rs. 2,155,500. This concession obtained after so much trouble and at so much expense was the coining of Rupees after the Arcot stamp. The Rupees were therefore issued neither in the name of the Company nor of the French Government, but in the name of successive Moghul Emperors from 1736 to 1839, even after the death of the last Moghul in 1806, the only distinctive feature being the appearance of a crescent by the side of the year of the reigning Emperor of Delhi similar to the star or flower of the same stamp found on the Arcot and Murshidabad Rupees of the British East India Company.

HINDUSTANI LEGEND :—

Obverse :—Rupee struck in the name of Mahomad Shah the 19th year from his accession the year 1149 of the Hijra Era.

Reverse :—Hindustani Legend :—

Blessed coin of the Victorious Emperor Muhammad then struck at Arcot the year 19 (crescent) from the beginning of the glorious reign.

Here are some examples of the legends found on these Rupees which illustrate alike the extent of the pretensions of the great Moghul and the need of the Christian Company which induced them to apparently recognize them. "The chosen of the faith struck money in the seven regions brilliant like the sun and the moon." "The Emperor Shah Alam, the shadow of excellence, ardent in the faith of Mahomet, has struck this money for the seven regions." "The father of justice, Shah Alangir, the Victorious Emperor, God grant his kingdom may endure."

The operations of the Pondichery mint thus far progressive and prosperous came soon to an untimely end. The occupation of the Pondichery settlement by the English from 1793 to 1816 led to the suspension of the working of the mint during that period. When the settlement was restored to the French in 1815, the Local Government less for fiscal than political reasons wanted to resume the coining of money. The chief object they had in view was to exercise a sovereign right regarded as an emblem of regal power by the Indian merchants who were incapable of viewing the renunciation of the privilege as voluntary or due to any cause except utter defeat and absolute loss of prestige. The local Government proceeded at once to reopen the Pondichery mint with beneficial consequences which they depicted in glowing terms to the authorities at home, adding that in no country was the force of custom and prejudice so potent as in India, an observation which is as true to-day as in the year 1815. The most important offices having been always held by Brahmins, the heads of two families still living had then the happiness of initiating their sons into the mysteries of coining pagodas, Rupees and *dudus* (copper coins).

A lengthy correspondence then ensued between the Pondichery and Madras Governments as to the intrinsic value and standard of these Rupees, but it was eventually recognised by the latter that the Pondichery rupee was the same or nearly the same as the Madras rupee, except for the mark of the crescent and that the intrinsic value of the former was slightly superior to that of the Madras rupee. Notwithstanding these circumstances apparently conducive to the prosperity of the French currency a new trouble came over the endeavours of the Local Government to restore its lost prestige. Ever paralysed by the action of the rival Government which, gradually introducing system and good order in its administration, had to prohibit the receipt of Pondichery rupees as legal tender in the Collector's treasuries, the operations of the French mint began to wane gradually and notwithstanding some spirited attempts to continue the currency, the mint had to be closed on 1st January 1840, and in 1871 all the coins issued by the French mint ceased to be legal currency.

And thus the national currency has disappeared from the capital of French India and the English currency has taken its place.

The settlements of Yanoan, Masulipatam, Mahe, Chandranagore and Surat had each their distinctive coinage. But there is something like morphology in coins and one could easily recognize the forms of a type, and judge therefrom alone that coins of a particular type had a common origin. The coins of the French wherever they were issued bore the impress of the Pondichery mint and could be easily classified as the coin of the French in India even by one who was not acquainted with the language in which the legends were inscribed. I shall therefore content myself with simply describing the coins issued for these settlements. *The Yanoan Pagoda* had on its obverse, three figures, standing Venkateswara and his two consorts, and on the reverse, on a granulated surface, the crescent as on the Pondichery Pagoda. The coin was minted at Pondichery for the use of the settlement of Yanaon.

Silver Rupees and copper *dubs* were coined for the *Settlement of Masulipatam,* 46 to 48 dubs having exchanged for a Rupee. The rupees were much like those of Pondichery and bore a Persian legend making it known that they were struck at Masulipatam in the regnal year of the ruling Moghul Emperor at Delhi. The distinctive mark of the Masulipatam rupee was a trident.

The copper *dubs* bore on the obverse the name of the Delhi Emperor and gave the year of his reign and on the reverse the legend Matchipathan and the regnal year. Rupees and *fanams* intended to meet the exigencies of the local currency of Mahe were struck at Pondichery. Though of the same fineness and weight, these coins were slightly broader than those intended for use in Pondichery, and were not received as legal tender in that settlement. Five of these *fanams* went to the Rupee and fifteen biches (paisas) in copper formed the value of each *fanam*. Half and quarter rupees as in Pondichery were also struck for Mahe.

The Mahe fanam had on its obverse a Hindustani legend in two lines "Fans Campanie" and on the reverse in two lines "Bhutcheri" P and the year of the Christian Era. The *Biches* bore on the obverse five fleur de lis and on the reverse the year of issue in the Christian Era.

The privilege of coining money in Bengal was obtained in 1739 by M. Dupliex and a thousand piastres were sent to Murshidabad for being converted into Rupees for the use *of the Settlement of Chandranagore.* The Rupees so struck were in the name of the reigning Emperor of Delhi giving his regnal year as in the Pondichery Rupees, but bore the distinguishing mark of a Jassamine flower. The denominations ranged from $\frac{1}{2}$ to $\frac{1}{64}$ of a Rupee.

In 1749 the privilege of coining rupees for the use of the factory of *Surat* was obtained from the Nawab of that place; these bore the words in Hindustani "struck at Surat" and gave the name of the reigning Emperor of Delhi with his regnal year and the date of Hijra Era.

The relations of the French with the great Tippu Sultan known as the Mysore Tiger, are illustrated by a curious medal which has on the obverse the inscription in Persian: The ambassadors of Tippu Saheb, the conqueror: Mahomad Dervish Khan, Akbar Alikhan and Muhammad Oosman Khan have met Louis XVI, King of the French, the 6th of the month Zelkadeh = 9 August 1788. On the reverse the legend runs: The three ambassadors have honoured with their visit the Royal mint of Paris on the 7th of the month Zihiadjeh = 9th September 1788.

I have thus attempted to give here a brief account of the French coinage in India. The operations of their mint were as ambitious as their plans for establishing a dominion in the East. It was a French General who first demonstrated that Indian Sepoys under European discipline would form fine fighting material; it was the same French General who proved that the determined attack of a well-organised handful of Europeans could withstand the resistance of undisciplined masses of which the then local armies were composed; his restless and ambitious propaganda for the extension and establishment of a French Empire did not however meet with that support and sympathy which his grand undertaking deserved. And what was the result? Let me give it in the words used by Major Malleson in 1868.

"But for one man the stake for which the two countries played would not have been so great. It was Dupleix who made French India, it was France who lost it. If in the present day, there exist amongst her citizens regrets at the loss of an Empire so vast, so powerful, so important, inhabited by a people who were civilized when we were naked savages, and who possess so many claims to the sympathy and attachment of every intelligent European, it will be impossible for France herself—however much she may condemn the action of her Government of those days, and may lament the infatuation and misconduct of her countrymen—to suppress a glow of pride at the recollection that it was a child of her soil who dared first to aspire to that great dominion, and that by means of the impulse which he gave, though followed out by his rivals, the inhabitants of Hindustan have become permanently united to their long parted kinsmen—the members of the great Family of Europe."

The Pallavas

The period of South Indian History between the second and tenth centuries of the Christian Era was an eventful one. It began with the downfall of the powerful Andhra dynasty which according to the Vishnu Purana had a rule of over four and a half centuries. It witnessed the decay of Budhhism, the extinction of Jainism and the revival of the Bhraminical faith in the forms in which it has continued to the present day. More than one powerful Empire rose and fell.

In this eventful period a race of immigrants played no insignificant part in building an Empire in that portion of the Madras Presidency which lies between the Godavari on the north, and the Pandyan boundary on the South with their three capitals Conjeeveram in the Chingleput District, Vengi in the Godavari District and Palghat in Malabar. They were, as early as the reign of the powerful Andhra king Vilivayakura II (A. D. 68-135) significant enough to engage in hostilities with him in Western India and were probably settled there as a ruling race long before they came into prominence as the Rulers of Thondainadu. They came in contact with the three great Kingdoms of the South—the Pandya, the Chola and the Chera, whom they claimed to have subjugated and were in personal hostility with the Chalukyas of the Dekhan and in evidence as an independent power till the time of the great Raja Raja Chola (985—1011).

The Ganga and Nolumba Pallavas who claimed kinship with the family of "Pallava Tilakas" carry the name of the Pallava race to a much later period and the present Thondaiman of the State of Pudukkottai still claims to be a "Raja Pallava.' The name Pallavaraya continues to be the tribal appellation of some of the Kallars of the Tanjore and Trichinopoly Districts, coupled or not with the title Tondaiman—"lord of Tondainadu."

Very little is known about the main Pallava dynasty except from the information furnished by the cave temples which they had excavated and embellished and the charters which they issued to evidence the grant of land for religious and charitable purposes. It is remarkable that a race, brave and adventurous, enjoying without doubt a high degree of civilisation, are now remembered only by the copperplates, lithic records and cave temples left by their Sovereigns.

The monolithic temples of Mamallapuram, on the coast, near Madras built by Narasimhavarman I and known as the seven Pagodas, still excite the admiration of the artist and the caves on the Trichinopoly Rock are fine specimens of the architecture of the times of Mahendravaram "Guna Bhara" more than thirteen centuries ago. These and other cave temples, found in the Southern Districts of the Presidency are distinctly characteristic of the architects who seem to have been adepts at fashioning huge boulders of rock into miniature temples and so working into the body of inaccessible rocks as to convert them into halls adorned with lifelike frescos representing scenes from the Indian Epic poems or the figures of the Gods taken from the

Hindu Pantheon. These cave temples however have no connection with the so called Panchapandava beds in caves and caverns which have been discovered in various parts of the Southern portion of the Peninsula.

The cave temples of the Pallavas were the natural successors of the earliest lithic monuments of the Tamil country, known as the Pancha Pandava beds which have been discovered in inaccessible natural caves, in the Madura and Tinnevelly Districts and the Island of Ceylon, which at one time is supposed to have formed a part of the main land under the name of Taprabone separated by the river Silon. These beds accompanied by inscriptions in the characters resembling those of the Asoka Edicts and roughly assignable to the 2nd century A.D., were probably made at a time when Pali was understood in the Pandyan country in the palmy days of Buddhism, and the stonebeds in cells of two caves and the absence of pillars in the halls are also indicative of their early position in the history of cave architecture. The beds and inscriptions of decidedly Buddhist origin in the extreme south of the Peninsula point to the undisputed fact that Buddhism held a very strong place in the religious faith and practices of the people in the centuries which preceded the predominence of the Pallavas.

The practice of so fitting caverns as to satisfy human needs by architecturally improving them, first adopted by the Buddhists was improved upon by the talented Pallavas and the result is that we have some of the noblest works of art in their cave temples, which have for over fourteen centuries, withstood the ravages of time, survived the wreck of mighty Empires and are today standing as monuments of a great and forgotten civilization. It is refreshing to note that the policy of religious toleration, pursued by the latest and greatest of Indian Empires was counted as of equal importance one thousand five hundred years ago when the figures and emblems of Brahma, Vishnu and Siva alike were carved, by the Pallava Empire builders, in their cave temples. And had the youngest religion of the world, the militant faith of Islam, been in evidence at the time, the crescent would have been quite as much honored and impartially assigned a place by the foreseeing Pallava Kings.

A brutal vandalism has in some cases been instrumental in mutilating, by chipping off the noses, the exquisite figures as in the Trichinopoly cave, but the scene of Arjuna's penance and the fine monolithic conception known as the Ganesh Temple in Mamallapuram still testify to the high standard of art which is the outstanding feature of Pallava architecture. In massiveness and imposing splendour the later Chola architecture and in wealth of detail that of the Chalukya temples of the Mysore Province may surpass the Pallava style, but the vigour and life of the Mammallapuram figures are not surpassed by them.

Various theories have been advanced about the origin of the Pallavas and the Puranic influence has not been slow to trace their origin to a mythical ancestor who had been nurtured on a bed of the tender sprouting leaves of a tree—the author of the idea having based it on the meaning conveyed by the Sanskrit word Pallava.

The theory that the Pallavas were probably the Parthivas who hailed from Persia and became knowns as 'Pahlavas' and 'Pallavas' is an alluring one. The high finish of their sculpture and the beautifully executed coins with the figures of the bull and the two-masted ship which abound in large numbers on the Coromandel Coast may perhaps lend colour to the theory. The bull itself was the emblem of the Pallava Kings, symbolised by that patience and assiduity which is so necessary for the achievement of greatness. The recumbent bull, facing the proper right, flanked on either side by two tall lamps—the symbols of light and truth—with other significant devices among which were the figure of 'Lakshmi' or the goddess of Prosperity and the Swastika, an honored symbol of justice and law: these are the emblems found on Pallava seals and coins. The conception of an obverse bearing these figures indicates a degree of civilization which must be counted as ancient as that of the times of Asoka and as high as that of any ideal which may be conceived by the human mind. The appearance of the two-masted ship on some of their coins attests to the seaborne trade between Persia and the Pallava country which seems to have been carried on in the prosperous days of the Pallava Kingdom.

The paucity of information connected with this interesting dynasty of kings is evidently not due to any absence of a desire on their part to leave indelible records of their doings. It is not often that we find a musical treatise on a rock and yet we have a long inscription in Kudumiyamalai in the Pudukkottai State engraved in Pallava-Grantha characters, divided into seven sections each of which professes to be a collection of musical "*svaras*". And sculptures accompanying the damaged Pallava epigraph in the Vaikuntha-Perumal temple were evidently intended to illustrate real historical events connected with the succession of Nandi-Varman after the death of the King Paramaswara-Varmen II, after the latter of whom probably the Temple was known as Paramesvara-Vinnagaram. The king to whom we owe the upper Trichinopoly cave seems to have left a statue of himself in one of the two niches, and in the other one of Iswara.

The history and chronology of a race of kings of the power and importance of the Pallavas cannot but be of great interest and full of lessons to every student of Indian History. The Velurpalayam plates of Ko Vijaya Nandivarman noticed in the Report of the Government Epigraphist issued along with G.O. No. 832 Public dated, 28th July 1911, has added materially to our knowledge of the later Pallavas whose main line had hitherto been supposed to end with Nandi Varman Pallavamalla, who was defeated by Vikramaditya II, the Chalukya King of Badami, and had to flee from the Pallava capital Conjivaram which fell into the hands of the enemy.

All the published Pallava grants begin by recounting the origin of the race from the lotus navel of Vishnu and bring the succession to the mythical Pallava nurtured on a litter of sprouts. Thereafter they give a geneology which, if partly based on tradition, is in the main of historic value.

It is the peculiar privilege of the East to express itself in tropes. The imagination which personified the dawn is present at every turn. A plain narrative of a succession of events was evidently too prosaic an achievement for the State scribe who composed a South Indian inscription.

This is the disconcerting factor in the equation of Indian Epigraphical studies. A Dravidian people whose vernacular was Telugu or Tamil must have their inscriptions in unspoken Sanskrit; the more modern, the less familiar was the language of the inscription. Every new race of kings which came into prominence wanted to trace its origin to the Sun and the Moon, the heroes of the Mahabharata, or a supernatural being. And poets were not wanting who could shed a halo round the crowned head of a hero. The student of history has to reckon with such recurring attitudes of mind and corresponding creations of the imagination in studying South Indian inscriptions which lay claim to trace the geneology of the kings under whose auspices they were issued. Imagination and tradition acted and reacted on each other. As a result we have a delicious jumble of a traditionary account embellished by the poet's frenzy. These remarks are suggested by the study of the inscriptions which pretend to give an apparently true account of the doings of a king whose religious benefaction is the immediate provocation for the composition of a seemingly historic narrative of his lineage and hereditary greatness. Such considerations as these are true of almost every South Indian inscription of note. Nor is the study of South Indian Numismatics of much value in matters relating to succession and chronology. With the characteristic indifference to such trifling details as dates or names the South Indian King rarely gave his true name on his coin if he gave it at all. Symbols and devices were used which very significantly portrayed the prevailing State religion. If a name appeared, it was applicable at least to half a dozen of the magnates of a particular line, who laid claim to martial prowess and universal dominion.

The evidence attended by such infirmative circumstunces it is that one has to examine before arriving at a tentative result in most matters relating to the history of South India in the eventful period of the first decade of the Christian Era.

The Velurpalayam copperplates are the latest discovery of the Government Epigraphical Department to whose activity we owe much of the meagre information that we have about the Pallavas. Till about seventy years ago nobody dreamed of assigning to them their proper place in South Indian History. Even at the present day their history till the end of the sixth century rests largely on conjecture.

A. Sivaskandavarman seems to have been powerful enough in the 2nd century A. D. to proclaim to his world that he had performed the Aswamedha-horse sacrifice. This was in Western India. It means that the Pallavas must have made their way into that portion of the country a good long time before the reign of the performer of the horse sacrifice. The hostilities of Vilivayakura were directed, we are told, against the Sakas, Yavanas and Pahlavas. The last named race was thus mentioned along with those foreign hordes who were regular thorns in the flesh of the powerful Andhra kings of Vishnupurana fame. When the Pallavas established their three dominions with capitals of a corresponding number it is not possible to even conjecture. They were perhaps driven from their home in Western India and in seeking a portion of the country beyond the influence of the waning but still powerful Andhra power, they moved further south and established themselves in their famous capital Conjeevaram.

The inscriptions furnish a long list of names from the time of the origin of the race from the navel of one of the Hindu Trinity till the time of the *Pallava* who came to be known as such because he spent his infant nurture on the cool bed of tender leafy sprouts. This is followed by a still longer list of the ancestors of the first king of whom we could not definitely predicate anything with historical certainty.

The historical student must be referred to the inscriptions themselves for detailed particulars of the traditionary accounts of the rise and progress of the Pallava kings. Many names of perhaps real live kings are given. But no attempt at chronological order seems to have been made in recounting the names and narrating the exploits of the kings who bore them.

For instance, reference is made to the conquest of Kanchi by a Pallava ruler of the Earth and the marriage of a very early Pallava to a Naga princess is adumbrated. Both these events are of great moment in Pallava history. The former should indicate, if fuller particulars were given, the true age of the advent and establishment as a conquering and dominant power of the Pallavas in the southern portion of the Peninsula. The latter should give us an idea as to the epoch when a foreign prince found it necessary and possible by education, experience and environments to effect a political alliance with an aboriginal princess of the Naga tribe. Yet the inscriptions could provide us with no clue as to the age of these momentous events.

Of the numerous descendants who followed in the wake of the mythical Pallava are mentioned Skandavarman, Kalindavarman, Kanagopa, Virakurcha, Virasimha, Simhavarman, Vishnusimha and others, as illustrious scions of the main line. There is every probability of these having been real rulers of the land. With regard to many of these we have no more information than that they had "joined the gods." But the details furnished by the Velurpalayam plates regarding some of the predecessors of Simhavishnu from whose time it is possible to construct a fairly regular geneological table, are illuminating. And I give them in the words of Mr. H. Krishna Sastri, in his interesting report as Assistant Archaeological Superintendent for epigraphy, Southern circle, in the year 1911. "Kalabhartri, who may perhaps be the same as Kanagopa of other inscriptions (the Sanskrit *bhartri* and *gopa* being synonymous) is the first king mentioned. He is stated only to have been the jewel of his race. His son was Chutapallava. From whom was born Virakurcha who acquired all the emblems of royalty on marrying the daughter of the lord of serpents—evidently a Naga princess. Then came Skandasishya 'who received the burden of (maintaining) the *ghatika* of Brahmanas from king Satyasena'. After him was born Kumaravishnu who took the town of Kanchi; and then came Budhavarman 'the submarine fire to the ocean of Chola forces.' Here comes a break in the succession and we are informed that several kings, including Vishnugopa, passed away before a certain Nandivarman I was born. This king, it is stated, caused by the favour of Siva the king of serpents named Drishtivisha (i.e. one who has poison in the eye) to dance.' After him came Simhavarama of great prowess and from whom was born the victorious Simhavishnu who conquered the Chola territory, which was resplendant with areca groves, was decorated by forests of paddy flats and sanctified by the (waters of the) daughter of Kavera (i e. the river Cauvery).'" After this the geneology is on firmer ground. And the royal pedigree from about the end of the sixth century A. D. to the end of the eighth century of the same era is brought down with certain additions and omissions to Nandivaram III, giving two new names after Nandivaram II (the Pallavamalla), viz. those of Dantivarman and Nandivarman III, to the table given by Mr. Vincent Smith. Speculation must be rife as to whether the Dantivarman and Nandivarman so added to the accepted geneology are the true princes of the main Pallava line or of those who merely claimed to be descended therefrom, there being known another set of Dantivarman and Nandivarman of the Bahur plates, and the names of Danti and Nandi being of common occurrence in the South Indian inscriptions of a later date than that of the latest discovery of the Government Epigraphical department. But there is every reason to believe that the added names are those of the scions of the main Pallava line. It is beyond the scope of this popular exposition to enter into the examination of the data supporting this conclusion. All that is attempted now is to create an interest in the examination of the original sources of Pallava history by giving a general outline of the information available so far.

The materials thus furnished by the above mentioned grant, which is a typical one, have to be compared and collated with those which can be gleaned from other charters of the Pallava Kings of which many are known and contemporaneous grants of princes of other lines of Indian kings. The early ones are in Prakrit. They give us the names of Sivaskandavarman, Vijiyaskandavarman, Vijaya Bhuda Varman and Bhudyankura. They all belonged to the Bharadvaja Gotra and must have been later than what time the Pallavas moved into Kanchi from their home in Western India And their territories seem to have comprised at this time not only the land of Kanchi but also a portion of the provinces which had acknowledged the sovereignty of the Andhras. By the time of Samudragupta's invasion of South India in the 4th century A.D. the Pallavas had their capitals in the three different provinces. That great monarch, after his successful campaigns, North, South, East and West, had his achievements recorded on a Stone Pillar set up by Asoka six centuries previously in Allahabad. Of the many chieftains who had been vanquished by him, are mentioned, Hastivarman of Vengi; Vishnugopa King of Kanchi; and a third chieftain, Ugrasena, King of Palakka. The Prakrit grants and the inscription of the Indian Napoleon after his tour of conquest are practically the materials for building up the history of the Pallavas in the 3rd and 4th centuries. Vishnugopa is mentioned in the typical grant of later times. But there is wanting the evidence to prove the age in which he had flourished. A Yuvaraja

Vishnugopa is mentioned in a later Sanskrit Charter. This was the heir-apparent, according to that record, of Skandavarman II, son of Viravarman and grandson of Skandavarman. Vishnugopa accordinng to traditional account seems to have 'joined the gods' before the first Nandivarman. The third Century A.D. is "one of the dark spaces in the spectum of Indian History and almost every event of that time is concealed from view by an impenetrable veil of oblivion." This is true of the history of the Pallavas in the centuries presiding Simhavishnu. Who was this Hastivarma of Vengi? Is he the King of Attivarma "who issued the undated grant in the Prakrit tongue which was found in the Guntur District"? And Ugrasena of Palghaut, who was of moment enough to attract the notice of the Empire builder, Samudragupta, who dreamed himself fit to engrave his sanguinary exploits on the same stone as whereon the Great Asoka had cut out his message of love to all things living: who was this Ugrasena of Malabar? Are the virile and handsome Nairs the representatives of the Parthivas and are their old-world marriage customs foreign to Bharatavarsha? These are considerations which present themselves to the baffled explorer in the virgin land of Indian History. The names themselves of the monarchs who must be assigned to these two centuries indicate a gradual change in the prevailing religion of the times: Skandavarman, Bhudha Varman and Vishnugopa are terms which to the cultured Indian, have their deep-rooted significance. Instinct and ratiocination ever waged their battles in the arena of religion with varying success. And it seems to have been so in a country in which the Chinese pilgrim Hiuen Tsang who visited

Kanchi two and a half centuries later found in the Pallava country hundreds of Sangharamas and thousands of Buddhist priests who studied the *Sthavira* School belonging to the Great Vehicle, side by side with many *Deva* temples and many heretics termed *Nigranthas.* In any notice of the Pallavas it must be borne in mind that they must have come into contact with the ancient civilisation of the three kings of the south, who eighteen hundred years ago had made it possible for the world to have such refined and artistic productions as the Silappadhikaram and Manimekhalai. Likewise note must be taken of that religious convulsion which, in the fulness of time enabled Sambhanda of a later period to effect the conversion of Kubja Pandya 'into a Ninra Sir Nedumaran' and the efforts of the reforming Vaishnava Alwars who side by side with the Saiva lyric poets and saints contributed not a little to shape the life and conduct of the people of this great Country. The Pallava kings who established themselves in South India probably about the end of the second or beginning of the third century A. D. were thus face to face with moral and religious ideals which, to orthodox but tolerant Hindus, as they seem to have been, were the invisible springs of the inspiration which embellished the exquisite monolithic structures they have left to an admiring posterity. At present we have no tangible facts giving us a definite idea as to the part they must assuredly have played in shaping our present inherited tendencies and beliefs.

In the attempt thus made to trace the rise and growth of the Pallavas as a ruling race during the first four centuries of the Christian Era the paucity of authentic records bearing on their history in those early centuries was indicated. Evidence is no doubt not wanting that they had established themselves in the modern Conjeevaram much before the 5th century A.D. and administered three separate provinces, which acknowledged the overlordship of perhaps the Pallava Emperor of Kanchi. The cloud which in this wise overhangs their early history is not dispelled to any appreciable extent till we reach the latter half of the seventh century.

The ancient records of the Pallavatilakas, the main Pallava line as distinguished from those who claimed kinship thereto, are represented by a few copper plate grants and not by lithic inscriptions. It is in the present state of epigraphical research not possible to make anything like an accurate historical survey of the period before the end of the sixth century, the time of Simhavishnu. The Sanskrit charters issued from Dasanapura, Palakkada and Menmatura in the 5th and 6th centuries give a pedigree commencing from Skandavarman, of which the grant of Pikiri, in the Mundarashtra country, is a typical instance, do not throw much light on early Pallava history.

The donor of the grant under reference, Simhavarman traces his geneology through his father *Yuvaraja* Vishnugopa, who evidently had died as heir-apparent as the term italicised indicates, to Skandavarman who was the grandson of Skandavarman. This Simhavarman was evidently the Simhavarman II who made the Mangadur grant from Dasanapura and the device adopted, as in the Uruvalli plates also from the Mundarashtra District, was a lioness. The Darsi grant from the Nellore District mentions a great grandson of Virakurcha referred to as one of the early Pallavas in the Velurpalayam plates adverted to already. The Mydavolu record of Sivaskandavaram probably belong to the same class, though the seal attached to it has a couchant bull as the dynastic device and the language used is Prakrit as in the Hiradagalli plates. It is significant that the records of this series do not refer to Kanchi as the place from which they were issued thus justifying the surmise of the late Rao Bahadur Venkiah that perhaps the territory around and including Kanchi was then temporarily in the occupation of an inimical power, probably the Cholas. These early Pallava kings belonged to the Bharadwaja Gotra and if all the achievements claimed for them were real, their predominence over a good portion of India, south of the Vindhyas, was already acknowledged. Where definite evidence is wanting it were useless to indulge in any speculation as to their religious faith or the part they played in shaping the civilization of their age. The Brahminic influence, it is certain, was felt then, as it is now, despite the attempt to stifle it, and in the end was victorious, in competition with those of the Buddhists and Jainas. This alone can be predicated with any definiteness.

From about the end of the sixth century however, an era opens itself in which we have something more tangible than conjecture to go upon. The lithic records have to be attributed to this period. Simhavishnu the first king of this series claims to have defeated the Sinhalese King of Ceylon and been victorious over the Chera, Chola and Pandya. Synchronous almost with the prominence of the Pallavas under Simhavishnu was their hostile contact with the rising Chalukya power, a hostility which was destined eventually to put an end to Pallava supremacy in Southern India and reduce the scions of this ancient dynasty to the humble position of generals or provincial governors under the Chola Kings. To Simhavishnu's son, Mahendravarman, we owe almost all the monolithic cave temples in the North Arcot, Chingleput, South Arcot and Trichy Districts with inscriptions giving one or other of his surnames, Gunabhara, Satrumalla, Narendra, Avani Bhajana, Bhuvanabhajana. As Gunabhara we know him in the monolithic temple on the bank of the tank near Mahendravadi in the North Arcot District as well as in the upper cave on the Trichinopoly Rock; as Narendra Satrumalla in the caves of Dalavanur in the South Arcot District; as Avani Bhajana in the rock-cut cave of Siyamangalam in the North Arcot District and as Bhuvana Bajana (*Bhuvana* and *avani* being synonymous) in the Vallam cave in the Chingleput District. A Tondaiman who had the wealth, power and importance to have brought into existence so many remarkable works of art and was probably responsible for some of the *Rathas* of the deservedly admired 'Seven Pagodas' should have been a monarch of no mean pretensions. The territories over which he ruled not only comprised the Tondaimandalam but also a portion of the ancient Chola territory. The martial exploits claimed for him of having vanquished the three Dravidian Kings of the South, the Chera, Chola and Pandya, and humbled the Chalukya King Pulakesin II could not be placed in the same category as the title for universal supremacy arrogated to, in not a few instances, by petty princes in the incessant struggle for dominion which for a good long time was destined to be the familiar feature of the History of the Southern portion of the Peninsula of India. There is however no doubt that in the perennial hostilities between the Chalukyas and Pallavas during Mahendra's reign the latter were not invariably victorious. A good portion of the Pallava territory around Vengi seems to have been in the occupation of the Chalukyas, at least temporarily, as a result of the reverses sustained by the Pallava army. Yet the arts of peace no less than of war must have been cultivated during Mahendra's rule. The accoutrements and adornments of the figures carved in the cave Temples, furnish an index to the dress of the age, which seems to have been those of a prosperous people. There was evidently then not that sharp division between the Saivites and Vishnavites which unfortunately exists now. The cave temples of Trichinopoly, Vallam, Siyamangalam and Dalavanaur were dedicated to Siva, that at Mahendravadi to Vishnu and the one at Mandagappattu to Brahma, Iswara and Vishnu. The conception and execution of the tall, handsome and stalwart figures carved out on the granite walls, for instance in the Trichinopoly cave, were only possible in a people who were statuesque and strong. If the Puranic gods and goddesses represented by the carvings in relief in these caves could at once appeal to the people of the age it is easy to see how firmly the Puranic religion had become fixed in the land. The skill displayed in the execution of the carvings was unlike that of any other epoch in South Indian art. They are true to nature; and there is no attempt to resort to crude and fantastic makeshifts to represent vigour or strength, subterfuges characteristic of the art of a later age.

Mahendravarman I was succeeded by Narasimhavarman under whom the Pallava power attained its zenith. The temporary defeats sustained by the father were more than made up for by the signal victory gained by the son in the hostilities which he, as a filial duty, directed against the Chalukyas, with the result that he took Vatapi, the Chalukya capital, from Pulakesin II. Narasimhan is referred to in later grants as the conqueror of Vatapi. He became practically the Lord of Southern India, ruled over a territory which according to Hieun Tsang who visited Kanchi during his reign in 640 A. D. was 'about a thousand miles in circuit' and assumed the title of Mahamalla.

The remains of a great city which became ruined many centuries ago, situated between Covelong and Sadras, known familiarly as the 'Seven Pagodas' to Europeans and Mahabalipuram to Indians, is referred to in Chola inscriptions as Mamallapuram, the city of Mahamalla. Many legends are current about the place and accounts are not wanting which make it the city of Mahabali to punish whose iniquities, Vishnu, one of the Hindu Trinity, assumed the form of a mortal dwarf and begged for a boon, which was granted by the impudent and unsuspecting Bali, of three feet of ground measured by the dwarf's feet and when the whole earth and heaven were encompassed by two of his feet, he claimed the third by placing his third foot on the head which was offered therefor by the Emperor who could not go back on his word and thus was crushed. The Bana chiefs claim to be descended from Mahabali himself but their connection with Mahabalipuram rests on fancy and no tangible proof. The inscriptions on the Rathas, such as Sribhara, Bhuvanabhajana and Narasimha clearly indicate the true history of the Rathas which were hewn out of stone during the palmy days of the Pallava rule and assumed their wondrous shapes by the toil of artists extending over probably more than a century. The city seems to have extended far east into the sea and what is known now the "Shore temple" as was probably quite in the centre of a magnificent group of sculptures, the greater portion of which was swallowed up by the encroaching waters at some period of which we have no record. It will be beyond the scope of this lecture to enlarge on the remarkable artistic monuments known as the 'Seven Pagodas.' All that need be emphasised here is that the specimens of architecture which have survived from the times of Narasimhavarman and his immediate successors, as the Mahabalipuram monoliths, are unique in that they indicate a period of transition between the style of art of the Buddhist times and that of the later conventional creations of the Chola renaissance.

Narasimha's immediate successor, Mahendra II seems to have done nothing of note beyond holding together the vast territory which he inherited.

Parameswara I, his successor, is referred to in the copper plate grants as "the destroyer of the Chalukya forces" and according to the Kuram plates defeated Vikramaditya I (Chalukya) in Peruvalanallur, though records are not wanting which claim a victory for Vikramaditya himself over the Pallavas of Kanchi.

Of Rajasimha, the son of Parameswara, we know that he had the Kailasanatha Temple built in Kanchi. Another son of Rajasimha, Parameswara II, seems to have built the Vaikuntaperumal Temple in the same place. On the death of Parameswara II the succession to the throne was probably determined by popular election, Nandivarman Pallavamalla, a scion of a collateral line, being so chosen. It was during the reign of Nandivarman Pallavamalla that the Chulukyas under Vikramaditya II claim a crushing defeat of the Pallavas and the downfall thus of Pallava supremacy. Dantivarman succeeded Pallavamalla and was probably the Aparajita who defeated the Pandyan Varaguna in the battle of Sripurambiya and Nandivarman succeeded Dantivarman. Dantivarman, though a Pallavamaharaja, is said to have married a Kadamba princess and his son Nadivarman, the donor of the Velurpalayam record, is said to have granted the village of Tirukkattuppalli at the request of a Kumarankusa, "the jewel of Chola race." No further light is thrown on the doings of the times of Danti and Nandi by epigraphy. This brings down the history of the main line to about the end of the eighth century. Thereafter the Pallavas lost their splendour, and their descendants became probably the feudatories of the rising Cholas.

The period covered by the growth and decline of the Pallavas, was one of the most momentous in South Indian History. Saiva and Vaishnava reformers and poets waged uncompromising war with the votaries of Buddhism and Jainism and practically exterminated them from the land. The output of scholastic and dialectic effort during this age resulted in the composition of the most ancient and classical portion of South Indian Literature. The system of Government devised by the Pallavas was one indicative of a fairly advanced civilization. And when we remember that the most admirable portion of South Indian sculptures are those coming from their times, we cannot resist the conclusion that they played no insignificant part in the development of the country and the construction of its ideals, religious and secular.

List of Pallava Coins in the Cabinet

OF

T. M. Rangachari and T. Desikachari

No. 1 COPPER

Obv: A standing maneless lion facing the right, within a circle.

Rev: Four dots within a lined circle.

Sir W. Elliot thought that similar specimens were standard weights from the number of dots on the reverse. The presence of the same number of dots on specimens of varying weight evidently having correlative values, tends to weaken the "weight" theory.

Elliot fig. N. G.* 103. N. O. fig. 58.

Bell-Progress Report 1882. pl. 7, fig. 13.

No. 2 COPPER

Obv: a maneless lion facing the right.

Rev: the four legs of an animal, perhaps a lion. (Obtained from the Madura District.)

No. 3 COPPER

Obv: a lion passant with an ample mane facing the right.

Rev: a vase probably intended to represent the *Kama kumbha* (or vass of plenty) flanked on each side by a standard or a sacrificial lamp. Above the vase, a symbol standing for the sun, and on either side

---

*. Numismatic Gleanings.

thereof, *chamaras*. Unlike the coins referred to in Elliot, this specimen is very thin.

Coins of a similar type have been attributed by Sir Walter Elliot to the Pallava dynasty. N. G. fig. 48, 49, 50, 52.

They were obtained by him from the Masulipatam District and attributed by him to the Pallava dynasty of Vengi. The specimen under notice was obtained at Kilakarai evidencing the predominance of the Pallava power in the extreme South of India. Unpublished.

No. 4 COPPER

Obv: a lion with an ample mane, passant right, facing the front, surrounded by an ornamental ring of dots.

Rev: the sacred wheel.

The coin is thicker than the last and is much eaten up by rust. Obtained from the Madura district. Uupublished.

No. 5 COPPER

Obv: Lion passant to the right surrounded by a dotted circle.

Rev: A four limbed *chakram* (?) Located in the angles between the limbs are devices one of which stands for the *sun* and another of them is intended to represent the *cresant*. Obtained from Kumbakonam. Unpublished.

No. 14 COPPER

A thin piece, oblong shaped.

Obverse: an elephant facing the left, followed by a horse. Above the elephant is a device that resembless the *lingam;* to the left of this device, is the faint impression of a dagger.

Rev: Lion passant, maneless, with uplifted tail c/f Fig. 54. N. G. Sir W. Elliot.

No. 6 COPPER

Obv: Bull facing the right; in the field above is an emblem which resembles the pointed forefinger of the human hand, flanked by banners.

Rev: a rayed wheel (chakram). Coins similar in type but bigger in size are figured by Sir W. Elliot, N. G. fig. 32. N. O. No. 79.

No. 7 COPPER

Similar to No. 6 but the emblems appearing in the field above the bull differ.

No. 8 COPPER

Obv: Standing bull, right; legend above............ The whole within a circular enclosure adorned by a ring of dots.

Rev: The Ganda Bherund a (?) within a circular rayed enclosure.

No. 9 COPPER

Same as last, but the legend appears to be different.

Coins similar in type to the last two coins are figured by Sir W. Elliot in N. O.* figs. 82 to 85. N. G. Nos. 35 to 36.

No. 10 COPPER

Obv: the figure of a bull, rudely executed; above it the sun and moon; the whole within a ringed enclosure and dotted circle.

---

* Numismata Orientalia.

Rev: A chank flanked by two tall lights the whole whithin a rayed circle. Sir. W. Elliot in his Numismatic Gleanings (Nos. 76 and 77) attributes coins of a similar type to the Vengi series. It is noteworthy that the coin under notice was obtained in the south.

No. 11 COPPER

Obv: The figure of a bull facing the right, well defined and artistically executed; the head however is not visible, the stamp having been evidently larger than the piece of metal used for receiving the impression.

Rev: a Madras dhonie (boat).

Fig 38 of Elliot N. O. figs. 81 and 88 N. G. The coin is very thin and much eaten up by rust. Ascribed by Elliot to the 7th or 8th century.

No. 12 COPPER

Similar to Nos. 6 and 7 supra but much smaller.

No. 13 COPPER

Obv: Four elephants surrounding a central circle, perhaps intended to represent *Lakshmi.* (the goddess of prosperity.)

Rev: A rayed *chakram* (sacred wheel), Sir W. Elliot makes mention of punch marked Coins in which more than one animal appears surrounding a central device or emblem. Nos. 34 to 36 of his Sinha type. No coin however with four elephants, all evidently impressed at the same time on the Coins, and not as in the Coins of Sir Walter Elliot, the rest of successive "punches", has hitherto been met with. This Coin was obtained from Kumbakonam.

No. 14 COPPER

Duplicate of 11.

No. 15.

Obv: Standing figure of horse facing the right; above the horse, the crescent and other emblems; a club or baton in front; the whole encircled by a ring of dots.

Rev: worn out—smooth.

No. 17 COPPER

Obv: Bull facing the proper right with legend above:

Rev: There is a device in the centre, resembling a chank, (Sir W. Elliot thinks it is a vase with reference to a similar device on a coin with a different obverse: figs. No. 49 and 50) between two lampstands or standards. These devices are surrounded by a rayed circle.

No. 18 ALLOY

Obv: A lion with an ample mane facing the right.

Rev: a chank (Turbinella Repa) or a vase (?) between two tall lampstands or standards, the whole within a circle of radiating lines: Sir W. E. No. fig 49.

No. 19 ALLOY

Similar to No. 18 but thicker.

No. 20 COPPER

Obv: bull facing the proper right surrounded by a line and a ring of dots above the emblem the legend.

Rev: The chank (?) between two tall standards or lamps. The whole enclosed by a lined circle and a ring of dots c/f Sir W. Elliot N. O. fig. 31.

No. 21 COPPER

Same as No. 20 but smaller.

No. 22 COPPER

Obv: bull facing the right within a lined circle.

Rev: The chank (?) between two lampstands, the whole surrounded by a rayed circle.

No. 23 COPPR

Obv: Elephant facing the proper left with a dagger or a standard in front, the whole within a ring of dots.

Rev: Lion passant to the proper left.

No. 24 COPPER

Thin piece.

Obv: Lioness standing facing the left.

Rev: Elephant passant left with emblems above.

LIST OF PALLAVA COINS

IN THE

Government Central Museum, Madras

AND IN THE CABINET OF

DR. J. R. HENDERSON

The Government Central Museum, Madras

Dr. J. R. Henderson kindly placed at my disposal the coins in the Government Central Museum and those belonging to him to enable me to prepare these lists. The reading of the legends givon by me is but tentative.

1. Obverse: Standing bull, facing the right, with legend above *Sri bhara*, the whole surrounded by a lined circle. Reverse: Single fish perpendicular within an ornamented circle.

2. Obverse: Standing bull as No. 1 with legend above *Sri nidhi*. The whole within a lined circle. Rev: Same as that of number 1.

3. Obv: Standing bull, above the bull is the legend *Sri nidhi*. Rev: Tortoise within an ornamental circle.

4. Obv: Elephant left, with Nagari legend above; *Paka Deva*. Rev: Lion with trappings.

This is not a Pallava coin.

5. Obv: standing bull right with legend above, *Sribhara*, all within a lined circle. Rev: four lined Chakram.

6. Obv: Same as last in bad preservation.

Rev: four lined Chakram.

7. Obv: Same as last.

Do.

8. A broken piece, part of a larger coin.

Rev: *Chaitya* on a platform.

Obv: Standing bull within lined circle, The Head and the devices above have disappeared with the broken portion.

9. A well executed bull with legend *Sri nidhi*, all within a lined circle.

Rev: An eight limbed *chakram* within an ornamental circular enclosure.

Of the two specimens in the cover, marked 9 one is duplicate of No. 8.

10. Obv: Bull right with legend above probably *Sri bhara.*

Rev: a sacrificial lamp with six arms flanked by a dagger on each side, all within a lined circle.

11. Same as last but badly worn.

Rev: Do.

12. Obv: Bull right within a lined circle with legend above indistinct.

Rev: a bow within a lined circle.

13. Same as No. 12, but with legand *Sri bhara.*

Rev: as on No. 12.

14. Obv: Bull right with legend *Sri nidhi*.	Rev: single fish within concentric lined and ornamented circle.
15. Obv: Bull right within an ornamental circle.	Rev: Doubtful device which looks like a fish.
16. Obv: Standing Bull with legend above *Sri bhara*.	Rev: an altar within a lined circle.
17. Obv: Standing bull right with legend indistinct.	Rev: an eight limbed Chakram within a circular ornanmental border.
18. Thick coin. Obv: standing bull right with legend above *manapara*.	Rev: The *chank* (turbinella rapa) on a pedastal within a rayed circle.
19. Obv: Standing bull right with emblems above.	Rev: The State Umbrella within a rayed circle.
20. Broken piece. Obv: Bull within a rayed enclosure.	Rev: Two fishes, within a rayed circle.
21. Broken piece. Legend *Sri bhara* abovo what was possibly a bull.	Rev: an eight limbed *chakram*.
22. Obv: Bull with legend above *Sri bhara* badly worn.	Rev: Two *chowries* or batons crossed within an ornamental circle
23. Obv: Bull right with legend above it, which is indistinct.	Rev: a *dagoba* within an ornamental circle.
24. Obv: Bull right with legend above *Srinidhi*.	Rev: a four limbed *chakram* within a rayed

inclosure with a *chaitya* in the angles formed by the limbs of the *chakram.*

25. Obv: Bull right with legend above *Sri bhara.* Rev: Eight limbed *chakram* within an ornamental circle.

all within a lined circle.

26. Obv: Bull right with legend above. Rev: as in No. 22.

27. Obv: Bull right. Rev: male and female figures within a rayed circle.

28. Obv: Bull right with legend *Sribha.* Rev: a *chaitya* within a circular ornamental enclosure.

a fine specimen.

29. Obv: Bull right, with doubtful legend above. Rev: Same ss No. 27.

30. Obv: Bull right with legend indistinct within a lined circle. Rev: Horse or lion within an ornamental enclosure.

31. Obv: standing bull right with indistinct legend above. Rev: Umbrella.

32. Obv: same as No. 31. Rev: a sixteen limbed Chakram.

33. Obv: standing bull right. Rev: within a lined circle is a device lika the Telugu letter Va.

Dr. J. R. Henderson

1.	Silver. Obv: Rudely executed bull with legend above.	Rev: The *chakram.*
2.	Silver. Obv: Bull right with legend above *Sribhara.*	Rev: Do.
3.	Obv: Bull right with legend above.	Rev: The *chank* within a lined circle.
4.	Bull right with legend above *Srinidhi.*	Rev: four limbed *chakram* with rays.
5.	Obv: Bull right with legend above, the whole within a lined circle.	Rev: Two *chowries* crossed.
6.	Obv: Bull—with doubtful devices or legend above.	Rev: The *Chaitya* within a lined circle.

Note.—Those which are not marked 'silver' are copper coins.

DRAVIDIAN COINS

BY

DEWAN BAHADUR T. M. RENGACHARIAR, B.A.

AND

DEWAN BAHADUR T. DESIKACHARIAR, B.A., B.L., M.R.A.S.

I

To trace the growth and development of the Monetary System in South India, we have to go back to the days of the Pandyas and the Cholas. Their coinage was mainly in copper and silver. Flat thin rectangular pieces in silver have been found both in Tinnevelly and Madura, bearing the impression of Buddhistic devices "punched" on them with a seal or seals. The appearance on their reverse of a symbol which forms the characteristic feature of the rectangular copper coins of Madura and Tinnevelly, point to the obvious inference that the coinage in both the metals is attributable to the same power, though the punch-marked silver coins must be assigned to an earlier age than that of the die-struck copper coins.

Similar coins in silver have been found in all parts of India. "They have been discovered among the ashes of the men who constructed the primitive tombs known as *kulis* (or kistaevens) of the south and unearthed from the ruins of buried cities in excavating the head waters of the Ganges Canal. In all parts, from the Sandarbans of the Ganges to the frontiers of Afghanistan they turn up from time to time." And more recently they have been reported to occur among the finds of the excavations in the ruined city of Anuradhapura in Ceylon.

From their occurrence over such a wide area and in such great number one might suppose that there was some uniform standard or unit of currency adopted everywhere in India. In the imperfect state of our knowledge of the ancient Indian Monetary System, no definite statement can be made about what exactly led to this apparent uniformity in the size and the devices of these coins. We can do no more than indicate the nature of the speculation on the subject leaving further research to throw more light on so obscure a topic.

The suggestion has often been advanced that the silver coins were the *purana* (ancient-elding) which formed the silver representative of the primitive seminal exponent of value named the *kalanju* approximately equal to 45 or 50 grains. There is no doubt of the existence of a certain relation between the weights and measures and the money of a country and the suggestion "that the monetary system of S. India is of indigenous origin based on rude, seminal and testaceous exponents of value which have been exchanged for definite metallic counters" has much to recommend it; but having regard to the varying weights of these silver pieces, it cannot be asserted as beyond doubt, that they represented the silver *kalanju*.

Another theory proceeds on the hypothesis that the Dravidians borrowed the Phœnician unit of the Drachma weighing 57 grains, which tallies with the weight of the punch-marked specimens obtained in Northern India. For many centuries before the Christian era, it is certain that Dravidian merchants had developed such a degree of maritime and commercial enterprise as to tempt them to undertake voyages across the seas to distant countries, and it is believed by some scholars that it was they, who becoming acquainted with an alphabetic writing derived from the Presemetic-Accadians north of the Euphrates valley, brought the script to India, being thus the first to introduce the art of writing into India. Such an adventurous people were not slow to introduce into their country, a metrical standard with which they became acquainted in their foreign transactions. "As the Phœnicians had penetrated everywhere establishing with their accustomed enterprise their factories on almost every coast, they soon discovered the metallic wealth of the land and began to work for the first time the veins of silver which had lain for ages unsuspected in the mountains." The silver plates from Tarshish were imported into India by the Phœnicians to buy Indian gold and in such transactions they must have adopted their own unit of the Drachma. It was not strange then that copying the example, the Tamils cut the silver sheets into small pieces, weighing approximately as much as the Phœnician unit and had the same passed as measures of value easily resolvable into a given quantity of gold. In course of time the silver pieces would come to be stamped with some authoritative mark or marks and with the change of the ruling power or the reception of a piece into the domains of another sovereign or through other causes, various seals would be imprint-

-ed on the same piece, in some instances one seal being superimposed over the other. This origin of the punch-marked silver coins at once explains the uniformity in size and the occurrence over such a wide area as from the Himalayas to Cape Comorin and the Island of Ceylon of the silver coins in question. They are supposed to have been the *Karshas* current at the time of Buddha, and the period of their currency synchronises with the palmy days of the Phœnician trade, six or seven centuries before the Christian era.

In a communication to the Royal Asiatic Society by Captain T. B. Jervis of the Engineer Corps in 1835, that talented Engineer essays to establish a relation between the *Massa* or *Masha* which is the basis of the *tola* and *seer* with the weight of a pound as deduced from a primitive universal standard, *viz.*, a pendulum vibrating seconds, one half of which roughly is the primitive cubit. "This pendulum cubed, and multiplied" into the weight of a cubic inch of distilled water, each cubic inch weighing 252 984 grains Troy, divided into 48 or 28 parts, furnishes an explanation of all the weights of whatever kind whether money or gross weight throughout the world in all ages." By a manipulation of the figures which it is needless here to reproduce, it is demonstrated that ancient *hun* or *pon* and a tenth of it the *fanam* were both multiples or sub-multiples of the *Massa* of 15 and odd grains each *hun* being also half of the Drachma of 109 grains.

Neither the weights of the punch-marked silver coins, nor those of the silver pieces of the period of the Chola ascendency, furnish any clue as to the correctness of any of these theories. The coins of Raja Raja weigh 90 grains; those of Uttama Chola 85 grains; and those of Kulothunga 70 grains.

We possess in the South India Inscriptions a fairly accurate record of the weights and measures current in the period after the 9th century A.D. during which the Cholas suddenly rose into prominence and were for a time supreme in Southern India.

An inscription in Mammalapuram (the Seven Pagodas) of the illustrious Ko Raja-raja Raja Kesari Varman, relating to a contract for the new division of their lands by the citizens of the town provides as follows :—

"Among those who are without land and are over the age of sixteen—from those who are engaged in trade half a *Kalanju* of gold (*pon*), from those who work for hire one-eighth of a *pon* and for (each) turn as ploughmen (?) three-eights of a (*pon*) shall be taken at the end of the year. From those who do not submit to this contract further twenty-five *Kalanjus* of gold shall be taken besides a fine. In an inscription of the Virupaksheswara Temple at Vembatu near Velur in the North Arcot District the value of property is calculated throughout in *Kula* pramanas or *Kulas* of gold (*pon*) and in *panas* and it is recorded that 242 *Kula* pramanas of gold and 41$\frac{1}{6}$ *panas* are equal to 36 *Kovais* of gold and 5$\frac{1}{8}$ *panas*.

In the Kanchipuram inscriptions of Madurai-Konda-Ko-parakesarivarman, we find the penalty for a person not carrying out a charitable obligation was the payment of "one *manjadi* of gold daily to the king who is then ruling" or "one-eighth of a *pon* daily paid in Court" or "one *Kunri* of gold daily paid in Court." In another inscription of the 3rd year of Ko Raja Kesarivarman, from the same place, it is recorded that the villagers of Manalur pledged themselves to furnish oil for a lamp from the interest of a sum of money received from the royal Treasury said to be "eighteen *Kalanju*, ten *Manjadis* and one *Kunri* of gold."

In the Raja Raja inscriptions of Tanjore the weight of the jewels presented to the Temple is expressed in *Kalanju*, *Manjadi* and *Kunri* according to standard weights made of stone and preserved in the shrine of the god Adavattan, also called Dakshina Meru Vitankar. Silver seems to have been also weighed in *Kalanjus* and *Manjadi* and rated just in the same way as gold and the precious stones and pearls. Copper seems to have been weighed in *palas*, a copper water pot (*kudam*) being recorded as weighing three thousand eighty three *palas*.

From other inscriptions we find that the gold *kasu* was half a *madurantaka madai*, that an *akkam* 1/12 of a *kasu*.

The purchasing power of a *kasu* is found to be 2 *kalams* of paddy or 3 sheep or 1200 plantains or 7/20 *Kalanju* of gold.

Besides the *madai*, the *kasu*, the *kovai* and the *akkam* reference is found to another term, signifying token or a weight, if not a coin, as in the instance of a payment of so many *Kanam* a day into court as a fine.

Moreover two kinds of *pons* are also referred to as "Urkkachchemmai—pon" and "tulainirai"—pon which are equivalents of so many kalanjus gold.

Whether there was any definite ratio between the value of gold and silver or whether the value of gold fluctuated with that of any other commodity and was determind in silver are matters upon which it would be rash to hazard even a conjecture.

The only Pandyan gold coin known to us is a tiny piece ascribable to "Sundara Pandya," but it is impossible to locate the age of the monarch who issued the coin. The period of Chola ascendency has examples of the coins of Raja Raja Chola in gold, and gold coins of more than one denomination in the Chola-Chalukyan period.

Side by side with coins or tokens in the precious metals the Pandyans possessed a currency in copper, which comprised die-struk coins unlike the punch-marked silver adverted to already. They resolve themselves into two varieties, rectangular coins which bear Buddhistic devices and a later variety of coins which are round and bear Vishnavite or Sivite emblems.

The former of the Buddhist coins occur at least in five denominations, the smallest weighing 30 grains while the heaviest coins weigh 144 grains, the intermediate weights are 40, 60 and 80 grains.

Writing about the economic conditions in Buddhist India, Professor Rhys Davids makes the following observations which are instructive in the investigation of this copper coinage. "The older system of traffic by barter had entirely passed away never to return. The latter system of a currency of standard and token coins issued and regulated by Government authority had not yet arisen. Transactions were carried on, values estimated, and bargains struck in terms of the *Kahapana*, a square copper coin weighing about 146 grains and guaranteed as to weight and fineness by punch-marks, by private individuals. Whether these punch-marks are tokens of merchants or of guilds or simply of the bullion dealer is not certain." These observations are of interest, relating as they do to the coins occurring in Northern India and based on the examination of the Buddhist records unconnected with the Tamils who, by the geographical position of their country, had for over twenty centuries maintained their political independence in the southernmost portion of the Peninsula. It is remarkable that as in the silver punch-marked coins the size, weight, and devices resemble very much those of the coins occurring in portions of India remote from Tamil Kingdom and having nothing in common except perhaps the religion of Buddha.

With the change in the shape of the old variety and the introduction of the symbols of a different faith, the practice of issuing "Kahapanas" of 144 grains was discontinued. The Monetary System seems to have been remodelled, and henceforth no silver coins were probably issued and coins in copper of various denominations judging by the weights of specimens now available were put in circulation. The average weights of the various sizes are 58, 30, 14 and 7⅙ grains.

Tho change from the square coinage of the Buddhist period to the latter round coinage with Vishnavite and Sivite emblems and the adoption of an apparently different standard of weight must have been brought about by causes that cannot solely be looked for, in the revival of the Puranic faith in India. In the early centuries of the Christian era there was a large influx of foreign merchants and a considerable quantity of Roman aurei and dinarii must have been imported by them into India for purposes of merchandise and indeed we read of gifts in dinarii for the maintenance of lamps in temples. Small copper coins were also locally minted by a colony or colonies of foreigners and it is not improbable that the change in the shape and weight of the coins of the Tamil Kings had some sort of connection with their intercourse with Rome.

Of the copper coins of the period of the Chola ascendency the most numerous are the copper *kasus* of Raja Raja which occur in three varieties, the heaviest of them weighing 90 grains. The coins of the Chola-Chalukyan period present yet a further change in the weights of the heaviest specimens which on an average weigh 74 grains.

It will be evident from an examination of the weights of the various copper coins found in S. India that the task of arriving at a uniform standard for them is by no means a safe or easy one. Various factors are calculated to introduce confusion in any speculation bearing on the matter not the least of which are the discrepancies in the weights of the coins of the several denominations viewed from the standpoint of any of the various theories put forward to explain and fix the primitive unit of currency. The mention of a *kasu*, a *panam* or a *pon* in Tamil literature and inscriptions is of little import as connoting the idea of any definite value as the use of words of similar significance, *viz*., the *purana swarana* and *hyranya* in ancient Sanskrit and Pali literature, with reference to the coins and tokens in the precious metals.

II. PANDIAN COINS

The Coin collector in South India cannot fail to be struck by the large variety of issues in copper that abound in such great number in and about the sites of the ancient Pandyan capitals of Korkai (Tinnevelly District) and Madura. Equally remarkable is the curious feature of the Pandyan coinage that silver coins were either never issued, or were issued so sparingly that they have not come down to us at all. It is however, not free from doubt whether the silver, irregularly shaped, punch-marked pieces often found along with Pandyan coins were current in the Pandyan Kingdom during the prevalence of Buddism in India. A not dissimilar paucity is observable in the silver currrency of the Vijayanagar Kingdom, the prolificness of whose gold issues, is testified to by the innumerable *pagodas* and half *pagodas* available in the market even at the present day, while not more than three or four silver 'Vijanagar,' possibly forgeries, are known to S. I. Numismatists.

Pandyan gold coins are met with but rarely and are generally ill-designed fanams bearing on the obverse the figure of a man and on the reverse the legend, which if complete, may be read as "Sundara Pandyan." The late Lieut. General Pearse in his papers bequeathed to the Government Central Museum gave the following description of a gold coin which he procured in the London Maket for sixteen shillings :-

Obverse:—Two fishes looking downwards on a fish lying horizontally: above is an alligator. Two standards or *dwaja stambas* or pillars of Victory are supprorters to the central design.

Reverse:—Three lines of old bold *nagari* characters which have not been read. Col. Mackenzie noticing a coin of the same description attributes it to the ancient Pandyas.

Similar coins were found in South Canara which were probably issued by a branch of the Pandyas who had settled there.

Judging from the small number of gold issues that have hitherto found their way into coin cabinets, it appears to be a fair inference to draw that the Pandyan kings issued comparatively fewer gold coins than other dynasties of the South. It cannot however be forgotten that the Pandyans virtually ceased to be a ruling power nearly 500 years ago, that in India there is always a tendency to send gold in every form into the melting pot for satisfying the demand for jewellery in the precious metal and that it was by no means improbable that during the Mohammadan interregnum in Malabar, (the old name for S. India) and the long Nayakka rule the gold coins of the Pandyan kings found their way into the goldsmith's crucible and graced in time as jewels the persons of the fair devotees of Meenakshi.

By far the most interesting issues of the Pandyan dynasty, are those in copper, which seem to have been struck in such abundant profusion that they are met with now, after the lapse of centuries, in the Madura country and are picked out of the bed of the Vaigai or the fields near Korkai after a shower of rain.

The fish was the emblem of the Pandyans just as the tiger was that of the Cholas, the bow of the Cheras and the boar of the Chalukyas. Those which appear to be the earliest issues do not bear the emblem of the fish, but are square pieces, bearing well executed figures of the elephant and, the bull, on their obverse associated with many devices peculiar to the Buddhist faith like the wheel, the sacred tree, the khumba and the chaitya while on their reverse there invariably appears a diagram, by some supposed to represent the plan of Madura Town with the river Vaigai. The mounted figures on the elephant on some of the coins and the artistic finish and the perfect form of the images in all of them cannot but lead to the conclusion that they belonged to a period when the Buddhist influence was felt strongly in the south and when with the impetus given to the contact with the Yavanas (Greeks and Romans) there arose a school of art noted alike for the accuracy of its design and the chastity of its subject.

To much the same period must be attributed those thin small copper coins found in great number in and around Madura, which by their type and the legend imperfectly dicipherable on a few of them, must be assigned a Roman origin. Though there have been finds of aurei and dinarii in many parts of South India, nowhere so far as we know, except in Madura and Ceylon, are these small copper pieces to be met with. Moreover it is noteworthy that, while the type of this thin copper coinage is distinct from that of the Roman Imperial coins discovered among the South Indian finds, there is at the same time no corresponding currency in gold and silver answering to the insignificant-looking copper pieces. It is believed therefore that these copper coins must have been minted locally to meet the exigencies of a colony of Roman merchants that had settled in or around Madura. It is fairly certain that Roman soldiers were employed as body guards by the Tamil kings and to keep the gates of the Fort of Madura. A force of Roman Cohorts was stationed on the Malabar Coast to protect their trade. The Romans are said to have built a temple of Augustus at *Muchiri*, and a colony of Yavana merchants had settled at a place called *Caveripaddinam* which was a great emporium of trade in the Eastern Coast. In such circumstances, it is no extravagant theory to advance, that these small coins must have been issued for use in a small settlement of foreign merchants that had been established near Madura, for facilitating the extensive trade with India that we know was carried on by them in the first centuries of the Christian era. Most of them bear on their obverse the head of the Emperor with a legend around, while the reverse bears a striking resemblance to the reverse of the coins of Constantine.

Only one copper coin of a different type was found and that, not at Madura but at Devipatnam, during a period of nearly twenty five years of coin-hunting in Southern India. The obverse of this specimen bears the head of a female figure, legend Europa Roma, while the reverse bears the figure of a she-wolf suckling, Romulus and Remus, the reputed founders of Rome. From its type and from place where it was found, it is unlikely that it was issued out of a local mint, but must have been a stray copper piece that found its way to India during the period when the trade between this country and the Roman Empire was in a flourishing state.

We next come to a series, which unmistakably bear the impress of the Pandyan mint, bearing as they do on their obverse the Pandyan emblem of the single or double fish. On coins of this series are generally found engraved in Tamil the names or *birudus* of the monarch in whose time the coin was issued.

These names or titles are:—

Avanipa Segaran
Avanipendiran
Kodandaraman
Sundara Pandyan
Kachi Valangum Perumal

The legends Avanipasekharan and Avanipendiran, are comparble with titles assumed by Sundara Pandya as 'Conqueror of the world.' The coins bearing these legends were probably issued by a Pandya king named Avanipasegaran Srivallabha mentioned in an inscription on a rock south of the rock cut Jaina Temple at Sittannavasal in the Pudukkottai State. The legend on the coin has been read as Avanipasekharan golaga but it is capable of being read also as 'Avanipasekharan Chola' and it is not improbable that in the perennial conflict between the Panyas and the Cholas, a Chola king secured a signal victory over the Pandyas and to mark the event issued coins with the Pandian crest which by right of conquest he became entitled to use.

The legend '*Kodandaraman*,' may perhaps refer to Sundara Pandiya Jatvarman who in the Srirangam and Jambukeswaram inscriptions had it recorded that he was a second Rama in plundering Ceylon. 'Sri Kodandaraman' was a son of the Chola king Parantaka I who in the early part of the tenth century, claims to have defeated the Pandya king Rajasimha and slew "in an instant, at the head of a battle, an immense army despatched by the Lord of Lanka." If Chola inscriptions speak true he also invaded Ceylon. And the suggestion is here hazarded that Parantaka's son was probably left to govern the vanquished Pandya's country and the coins were issued to commemorate this remarkable event in Parantaka's reign. It was certainly the practice in those times in South India to issue coins or medals to mark a notable achievement of a monarch as illustrated by the legend 'Kachi Valangum Perumal,' literally meaning the king who gave back Conjiveram, commemorating a remarkable act of generosity even in Sundara Pandiya's age; the monarch, who conquered the Chola country generously restored it to the Chola king. These coins are of at least four varieties and some of them have the Tamil syllable "Su" on the obverse thus giving us a clue also to the name (Sundara Pandya) of the king who issued them.

The legend of Sundara Pandiya occurs in such a large number and variety of coins that it is hopeless to identify them with the reign of any particular monarch, though it may be fairly assumed that issues of Sundara Pandiya bearing the fish mark, were anterior to the period when Lankapura Dandanada according to the Mahavan so ordered that the Kahapana of Parakramabahu should be current in the Pandiyan kingdom. For after this edict, the obverse on the Pandiyan coins seems to have almost always become the figure of a Rakshasa or king, the rudely executed figure familiar to collectors of Sinhalese coins. By the time of Raja Raja Chola the "Ceylon Man," as this characteristic figure is generally known to South Indian Numismatists, seems to have been quite a familiar figure on the obverse of the Chola coins. What led to the adoption of this device by Raja Raja, the greatest monarch of his age, in supersession of the usual emblems found on Chola seals and coins of certain date, *viz*., the fish, bow and the tiger, it is not possible to definitely affirm. But it is enough here to note that the coins of the Pandiyan kings continued to bear the fish mark alone till a particular period and it may not be amiss to place the period in the middle of the 13th century.

We next have to deal with a series, in which the place of the fish on the obverse is taken by the Chalukyan emblem of the boar. The legend on the reverse is usually 'Sundara Pandya.' The boar, from which all gold coins, have got the name of *Varaha*, was a favourite emblem with more than one dynasty and a familiar instance of this is the appearance of the emblem on the Vijayanagara coins of Tirumalaroya. The Pandyan coins, with the boar obverse, have always the legend 'Sundara' on their reverse; there is no clue whereby we can attribute them to any particular reign. The boar emblem was probably assumed on an intermarriage between the Chalukya and Pandiya kings or on a conquest of the Chalukyas by the Pandyas.

The legend 'Sundara' is not confined to coins bearing the fish and boar emblems alone, but is found on those bearing on the obverse, 'the Ceylon Man' or a standing figure with hands folded as in the act of worship of a Hindu devotee. The variety of coins, obviously belonging to different times, which bear the legend 'Sundara,' furnishes yet another argument in support of the position already advanced on the strength of the recitals in inscriptions, that there were many Sundara Pandyas holding sway in the Pandyan country.

The coins of Vira Pandya also bear the figure of the "Ceylon Man" on their obverse. This Vira Pandya evidently ruled after the 1st war of the Pandyan succession and after the edict issued by Lankapura Dandanada that Parakrama Bahu's Kahapana which bore the figure of the "Ceylon Man" should be used throughout the conquered country. It is only natural that out of respect to the power that was instrumental in restoring Vira Pandya's father to the throne, he should try to compliment his benefactors by using the device of the 'Ceylon Man' on Pandyan coins.

Coins with the legends, Butala Viran, Ellamtalayanan, Kaliyuga Raman, Chonadu-Kondan, Cherakula Raman, also bear on their obverse the same device,, 'the Ceylon Man.' These legends do not indicate any particular sovereign in whose reign the coin bearing each legend was issued, but merely the title each sovereign assumed by reason of the exploit he believed he had achieved. Thus 'Butala Viran,' and

Ellam-talayanan signify that the monarchs, who assumed those titles, believed themselves to have been the only supreme warriors on the face of the earth or became the lord of all the mundane rulers. The coins of Ellam-talayam have on some of them the syllable 'Su' probably indicating the name Sundara Pandya.

'Chonadu Kondan,' conqueror of the Chola country, commemorates, perhaps, a victory gained by a Pandya king in the never-ceasing feuds between the two great Tamil Kingdoms.

"Kaliyugaraman and Cherakularaman" point possibly to the same facts as those recorded in the Srirangam inscription or to a second invasion of Ceylon, by the allied armies of the Pandyas and Cheras. But a Maravarman Tirunelveli Perumal Vira Pandya has inscriptions of his in the Ramnad and Tinnevelly Districts and the lithic records in the latter District mention coins known as those of Kaliyugaraman. The coins bearing this legend have therefore to be attributed to one of the later Pandyas who probably ruled in the 15th century. 'Kulasekhara' might stand for one of the many kings of that name who, associated almost always with a Sundara Pandyan, ruled over the Pandyan country.

The coins found in Madura are generally of a different type from those which are found in the Tinnevelly District. The latter are thicker in size, of a bolder type and invariably bear on the obverse the figure of 'the Ceylon Man.' Most of these have no legend imprinted on them, but have various devices of gods and demigods from the Hindu Pantheon, associated along with a battle axe, features wholly unfamiliar in the Madura Pandyan coins. The legends that they bear are, Sundara Pandya, Kulasekhara Pandya, or Vira Pandya, names which occur in the inscription of the later Pandyas in the Tinnevelly District.

Notwithstanding this dissimilarity between the two types of coins, even the casual observer can detect a family resemblance between them and there can be no doubt whatever, that the coins were issued by the scions of the ancient line, who after their real power was lost, retained still the vestige of sovereignty in the limited territory acknowledging their sway.

The next variety of Madura coins assignable to the Pandyan Kingdom are those with the legends:—

Samarakolahalan

Konerirayan

Bhuvaneka Viran

The coins with the legend Samarakolahalan are of various types, the most ordinary of which is that with the figure on the obverse of a *Garuda* (the anthropoid kite) now treading on a fish, now holding a *Vimana*, possibly the representation of the *Vimana* which was covered with gold at Srirangam by a great ancestor Jatavarman Sundara Pandya. The traditional lists have a Samarakolahalan, but the date of that king must be much earlier than the period to which the coins in question must be attributed. During the period of these later Pandya Kings the Nayaka Viceroys of Vijayanagar were practically the rulers of the Madura country and the dominion of the Pandyan must have been very similar to that of one of the big Zamindars of modern times. Yet the Pandyan was allowed to issue his own money. A Pandyan king named Tribhuvana Chakravarthi Konerinmai-Kondan is responsible for an inscription in the South Arcot district and registers by it an endowment for celebrating a festival called 'Buvanekaviran Sandi.' And an inscription on the Ekambaranatha temple in Conjiveram is said to have been made under the direction of a Bhuvaneka Viran Samarakolahalan dated A.D. 1469. The Konerinmai Kondan above referred to was probably the successor of this Samarakolahalan, and thus we have some authentic information of the sovereigns who probably issued the coins with these legends which abound in such large variety and number in the Southern Districts. The rule of the Nayakka was probably in the name of the titular Pandyan king and it is not unlikely that the coins were issued by the Naicks themselves in the name of the Pandyas, as in a later age the British East India Company struck coins with the effigy of Vishnu or in the name of Shah Alum.

The coins with the legend Koneriroyan have on their obverse the figure of a bull, and are very similar in type to the coins of the Vijayanagar dynasty. The title Bhuvaneka Viran, 'literally the only warrior in the whole world' is very much like the title Bhutala Viran and inscriptions of the sixteenth century of kings with the title Bhutala Vira were discovered near Kaniyakumari. With the type of coins just noticed comes to an end, the list of Pandyan coins discovered up to date. Coins of a later time, issued during the Nayaka rule, bearing the names of Visvanada and his successors, sometimes also having the name of the presiding deity of the Madura Temple or the name of the town itself in Tamil and Telegu, occur in large numbers but they bear upon Pandyan history if at all, in a very remote manner and therefore are omitted from consideration. From the brief survey made of the coins that may be attributed with a fair amount of certainty to the Pandyan kings, it is found that except the very old coins issued possibly during the first centuries of the Christian era, when Buddhism was the state religion in the south as it was in the north, the coins unearthed till now belong to the period between the 9th and 14th centuries A.D.

PLATE I

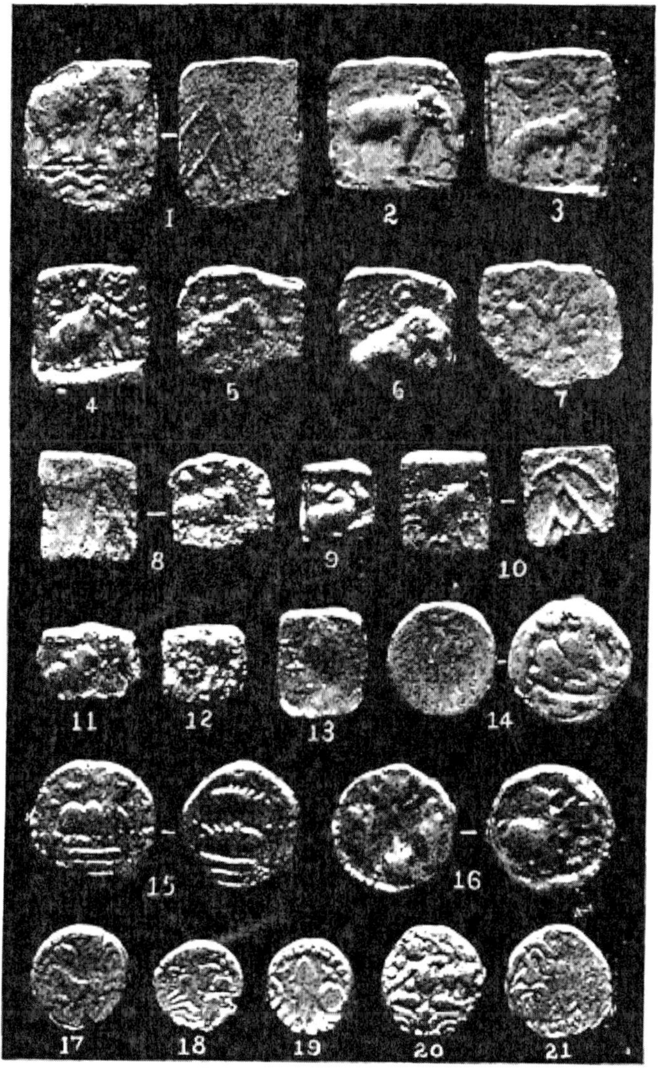

LIST OF PANDIYAN COINS

PLATE I

Fig. 1 A. E. *Obverse* :—Elephant facing the right, with a *Chaitya* in front.

Reverse :—A triangular diagram, with a wavy line above.

Fig. 2 A. E. *Obverse* :—Elephant facing the right, ridden by a warrior or a king with the mahout in front.

Reverse :—Same as fig. 1.

Fig. 3 A. E. *Obverse* :—Elephant facing the right with riders as in fig. 2 and two standing figures in front of the elephant.

Reverse :—Same as fig. 1.

Fig. 4 A. E. *Obverse* :—Elephant facing the right with riders and standing human figures as in fig. 3 together with a well executed *chakram* (the sacred wheel), in the field above the standing figure.

Reverse :—Same as fig. 1.

Fig. 5 A. E. *Obverse* :—Same as fig. 3 with Buddhist symbols above the elephant.

Reverse :—Same as fig. 1.

Fig. 6 A. E. *Obverse* :—Elephant with the *chakram* (the sacred wheel) and the *kumbham* (the sacred pot) above.

Reverse :—Same as fig. 1.

Fig. 7 A. E. *Obverse* :—The sacred tree of the Buddhists and other emblems.

Reverse :—Same as fig. 1.

Fig. 8 A. E. *Obverse* :—Bull advancing to the right, with the sacred tree in front and the sun and moon above.

Reverse :—Same as fig. 1.

Fig. 9 A. E. *Obverse* :—Bull advancing to the right, with the crescent in the field above.

Reverse :—Same as fig. 1.

Fig. 10 A. E. *Obverse* :—Bull advancing to the right.

Reverse :—Same as fig. 1.

Fig. 11 A. E. *Obverse* :—Bull passant with the sacred tree in front.

Reverse :—Same as fig. 1.

Fig. 12 A. E. *Obverse* :—The Buddhist symbols, *chakram*, *chaitya* and the elephant.

Reverse :—Same as fig. 1.

Fig. 13 A. E. *Obverse* :—Single fish in a perpendicular position with a lamp or standard by its side.

Reverse :—Defaced.

Fig. 14 A. E. *Obverse* :—Three fishes, with the crescent above.

Reverse :—Recumbent bull with the crescent above.

Fig. 15 A. E. *Obverse* :—Recumbent bull with the *trisul* in front and the crescent above.

Reverse :—Two fishes flanked by sacrificial lamps.

Fig. 16 A. E. *Obverse* :—Two fishes separated by a tall standard or umbrella.

Reverse :—Recumbent bull, right, with the crescent above.

Fig. 17 A. E. *Obverse* :—Maneless lion passant to the left with two fishes separated by a sceptre above.

Reverse :—Standing figure of a King in his regal robes, (as is fig. 46) which is the characteristic feature of the reverse of the coins of the Sinhalese Kings of Ceylon.

Fig. 18 A. E. *Obverse* :—A seated figure with that of a fish to its left.

Reverse :—Same as in fig. 17.

Fig. 19 A. E. *Obverse* :—Single fish between the sun and the crescent moon.

Reverse :—Same as in fig. 17.

Fig. 20 A. E. *Obverse* :—Seated figure with two fishes to its left.

Reverse :—Same as in fig. 17.

Fig. 21 A. E. *Obverse* and *Reverse*:—Same as fig. 20 but of a different type.

PLATE II

Fig. 24 A. E. *Obverse*:—Two fishes separated by a sceptre with the crescent above.

Reverse:—The Tamil legend: கோதண்ட ராமன் (Kodandaraman) with the state umbrella flanked by flags.

Fig. 23 A. E. *Obverse*:—The *vishnupada* (feet of Vishnu) with the 'chank' (conch shell) to the left of the central device and the state umbrella flanked by flags above.

Reverse:—Below the state umbrella flanked by flags is the Tamil legend கலியுகராமன் (Kaliyugaraman).

Fig. 24 A. E. Variant of fig. 23.

Fig. 25 A. E. *Obverse*:—Standing figure in regal robes with two fishes separated by a sceptre to its right.

Reverse:—Seated figure with legend to its left ஜெகவீர (Jagavira).

Fig. 26 A. E. *Obverse*:—Standing figure facing the left, with two fishes separated by a sceptre to the left of a standing figure;

PLATE II

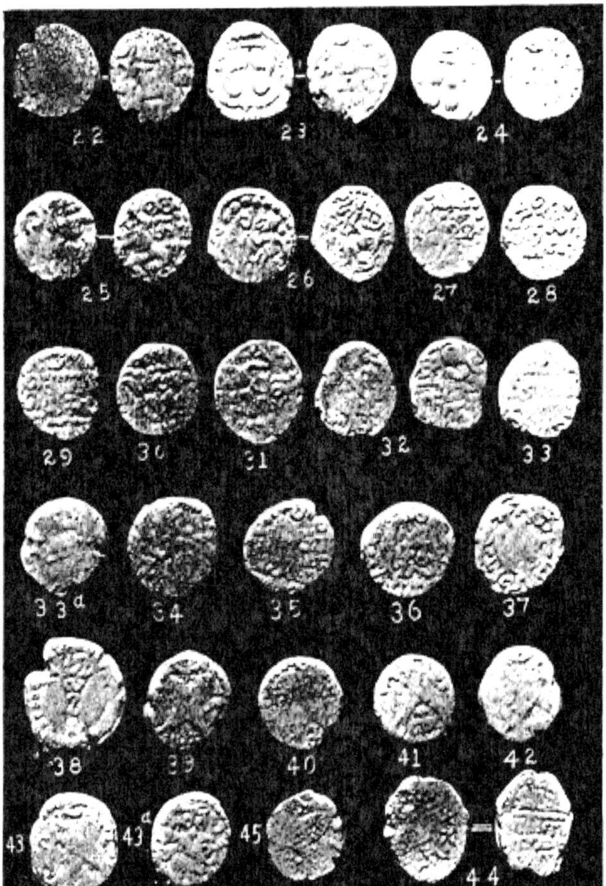
22
23
24
25
26
27
28
29
30
31
32
33
33a
34
35
36
37
38
39
40
41
42
43
43a
45
44

the whole surrounded by a ring of dots.

Reverse :—Seated figure facing the left with the Tamil legend ஜெக வீர (Jegavira).

Fig. 27 A. E. *Obverse* :—Variant of fig. 25. Standing figure with a lamp to its left.

Reverse :—Seated figure with legend in Tamil to its left பூதலவி (Butalavi).

Fig. 28 A. E. *Obverse* :—Standing figure with a lamp to its left.

Reverse :—Seated figure with Tamil legend சேரகுலராமன் (Cherakularaman).

Fig. 29 A. E. *Obverse* :—Standing figure in regal robes, as in fig. 46.

Reverse :—Tamil legend சோணாடுகொண்டான் 'Chonadukondan' or 'Cheranadukondan.'

Fig. 30 A. E. *Obverse* :—Standing figure in regal robes, as in fig. 46.

Reverse :—Seated figure of King with Tamil legend to its left பூதல (Butala) and two fishes below the legend.

Fig. 31 A. E. *Obverse* :—Standing figure in regal robes, as in fig. 46.

Reverse :—Seated figuro of King with Tamil legend to its left பூதல (Butala).

Fig. 32 A. E. *Obverse* :—Single fish flanked by lamps or standards with the state umbrella above.

Reverse :—Tamil legend அவனிபேந்திரன் (Avanipendiran) with the state umbrella flanked by flags above.

Figs. 33 & 33*a* A. E. Fig. 33*a* *Obverse* :—A tree on a pedestal with a bull below.

Fig. 33. *Reverse* :—Tamil legend அவனிபேந்திரன் (?) (Avanipendiran ?)

Fig. 34 A. E. *Obverse* :—Standing figure in regal robes, as in fig. 46.

Reverse :—Tamil legend எல்லாந்தலை (Ellanthalai).

Fig. 35 A. E. *Obverse* :—Standing figure in regal robes, as in fig. 46.

Reverse :—Single fish flanked by lamps or standards with the Tamil legend around எல்லாந்தலையாளுன் (Ellantalaiyanan).

Fig. 36 A. E. *Obverse* :—Standing figure as in fig. 35.

Reverse :—The Tamil legend எல்லாந்தலையாளுன் (Ellantalaiyanan) between two fishes.

Fig. 37 A. E. *Obverse* :—Standing figure as in fig. 46.

Reverse :—The same legend as in 35 surrounding two fishes in the centre.

Fig. 38 Variant of fig. 36.

PLATE III

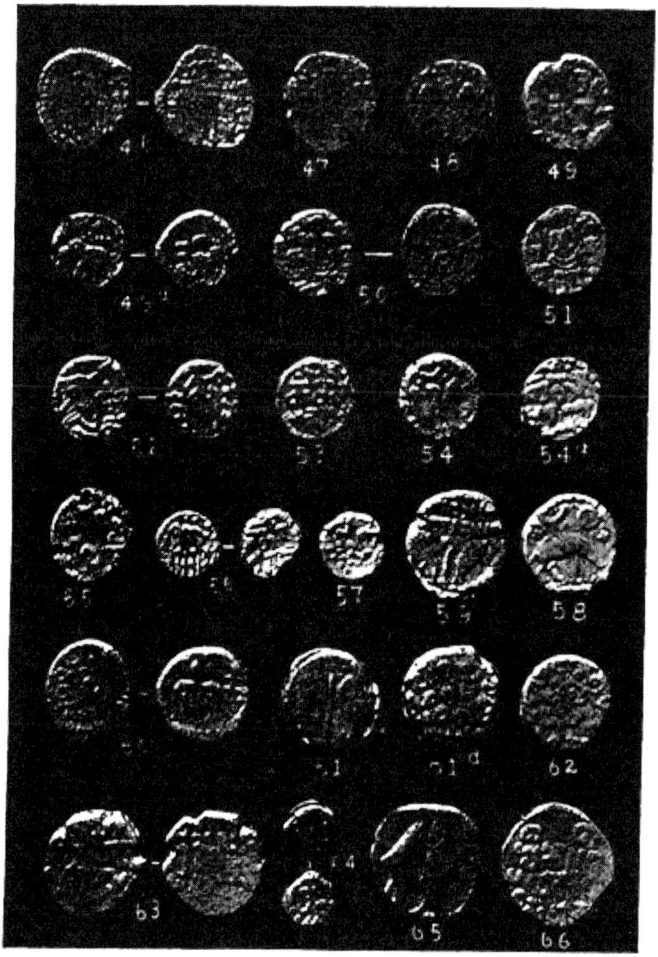

Fig. 39, „ 40, „ 41, „ 42, „ 43 — Two fishes crosswise, with the following emblems appearing in a different order in each different issue in the angles formed by the intersection of the fishes:—the *chank*, the sceptre, the trident, the crescent, and the Tamil syllable சு (su).

Fig. 43*a* — The Tamil legend கச்சிவழங்கும் பெருமாள் (Kacchivalangumperumal.) This is the legend on the reverse of all the figures Nos. 39 to 43.

Fig. 44 A. E. *Obverse*:—Two fishes crosswise below the crescent moon, with doubtful emblems in the angles.

Reverse:—கணிய. வி. பெ.

Fig. 45 A. E. *Obverse*:—Two fishes crosswise, below the crescent moon, with stars in the field to the left of the principal device.

Reverse:—Below the state umbrella, flanked by *chowries* or flags, is the Tamil legend similar to that in fig. 44.

PLATE III

Fig. 46 A. E. *Obverse*:—Standing figure of King in regal robes.

Reverse:—Two fishes separated by a sceptre and flanked by lamps or standards, with the Tamil legend வீரபாண்டியன் (Vira Pandiyan).

Fig. 47 A. E. *Obverse* :—Same as in fig. 46.

Reverse :—Same reverse as fig. 46, but of a different type.

Fig. 48 A. E. *Obverse* :—Same as No. 46.

Reverse :—Two fishes separated by a sceptre and flanked by lamps with Tamil legend above வீரபா—(Vira pa.)

Fig. 49 A. E. *Obverse* :—Standing figure of King in regal robes.

Reverse :—Above two fishes separated by a crook or a sceptre, the Tamil legend குலசேகரன் (Kulasekaran).

Fig. 49*a* A. E. *Obverse* :—Elephant passant to the left, with emblems or characters above, which cannot be deciphered.

Reverse :—Above two fishes separated by a sceptre is the Tamil legend குலசேகரன் (Kulasekaran).

Figs. 50 & 51 A. E. *Obverse* :—Standing figure with hands joined as in the act of worship with the legend in Tamil distributed on either side of the figure : சுந்தர பாண்டியன்.

Reverse:—Two fishes separated by a sceptre: above this device is the state umbrella flanked by flags.

Fig. 52 A. E. *Obverse*:—Standing figure of King arrayed in regal robes.

Reverse:—Seated figure similarly clad with legend in Tamil to its left: சுந்த: (Sunda).

Figs. 53, 54*a* & 55 A. E. *Obverse*:—Two fishes separated by a sceptre with the crescent above as in fig. 54.

Reverse:—Tamil legend சுந்தரபாண்டியன் (Sundara Pandyan) as in figs. 53, 54*a* and 55.

Figs. 56, 57 & 64 A. E. *Obverse*:—Standing figure of king clad in regal robes, as in 56 and 64.

Reverse:—Tamil legend சுந்தர பாண்டியன் (Sundara Pandyan) as in 56, 57 and 64.

Fig. 58 A. E. *Obverse*:—Boar facing the right on a pedestal with the sun and the crescent moon above.

Fig. 59 *Reverse* of fig. 58:—Two fishes separated by a sceptre with legend in Tamil சுந்தர பாண்டியன் (Sundara Pandyan).

Fig. 60 A. E. Same *Obverse* and *Reverse* as in fig. 56.

Fig. 61 & 62 A. E. *Obverse* :—Two fishes separated by an umbrella, as in 61.

Reverse :—Tamil legend..., வேமபெருமாள் (Vemaperumal), as in 61a and 62.

Fig. 63 A. E. *Obverse* :—Single fish flanked by lamps or standards with the state umbrella above.

Reverse :—Below the state umbrella flanked by flags is the Tamil legend அவனிபேந்திரன் (Avanipendiran).

Fig. 65, 66 A. E. *Obverse* :—Two fishes in a perpendicular position. Fig. 65.

Reverse :—Tamil legend ஸ்ரீ அவனிபசேகர கோளகன் (Sri Avanipa Sekara Kolakan) (fig. 66) c/o figs. 32 to 33a.

PLATE IV

Fig. 67 A. E. *Obverse* :—Seated figure with single fish to its left.

Reverse :—Tamil legend வீரபா (Virapa ?)

Fig. 68 A. E. *Obverse* :—Two fishes separated by a sceptre.

Reverse :—Tamil legend.

Fig. 69 & 70 A. E. *Obverse* :—Standing figure of King.

Reverse :—Two fishes separated by a dagger with Tamil legend விஸ்வநாதன் (Visvanadan).

PLATE IV

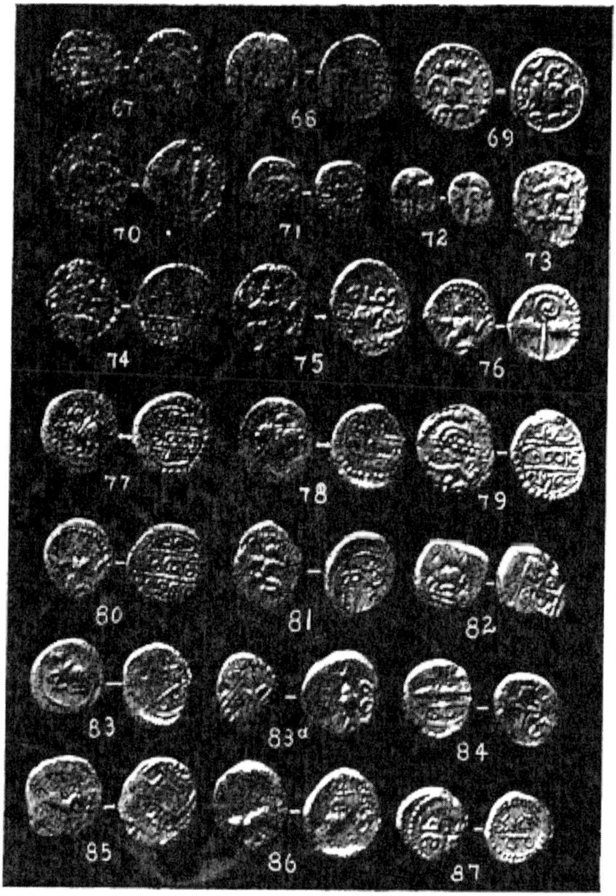

Fig. 71 A. E. *Obverse*:—Standing Ceylon figure.

Reverse:—Below the state umbrella flanked by *chowries*, is the Tamil legend:—குலசேகரன்.

Fig. 72 A. E. *Obverse*:—Standing Ceylon figure.

Reverse:—Two fishes separated by a sceptre.

Fig. 73 A. E. *Obverse*:—The anthropoid kite (*garuda*) with wings extended, and bearing the *chank* and *chakra*. (conch and discus).

Reverse:—The Tamil legend சமரகோலாகலன் (Samarakolakalan) as in fig. 74.

Fig. 74 A. E. *Obverse*:—The anthropoid kite as in fig. 73, above a fish.

Reverse:—The Tamil legend சமரகோலாகலன் (Samarakolakalan).

Fig. 75 A. E. *Obverse*:—The anthropoid kite as in fig. 73.

Reverse:—Tamil legend சமரகோலாகலன் (Samarakolakalan.)

Fig. 76 A. E. *Obverse*:—The anthropoid kite.

Reverse:—Two fishes separated by sceptre.

Fig. 77 A. E. *Obverse*:—Bull passant facing the left with a dagger in front.

Reverse:—Tamil legend கோனேரி (ராயன் ?)

Fig. 78 A. E. *Obverse*:—Bull passant to the left, bearing the state umbrella.

Reverse :—The Tamil legend கோனேரி ராயன் a dagger separating the legend.

Fig. 79 A. E. *Obverse* :—The anthropoid kite beneath an ornamented canopy.

Reverse :—Tamil legend புவனேகவீரன். (Buvanekaviran.)

Fig. 80 A. E. *Obverse* :—The anthropoid kite.

Reverse :—Tamil legend :—புவனேகவீரன்.

Fig. 81 A. E. *Obverse* :—Dancing figure.

Reverse :—Tamil legend மதுரை, (Madurai.)

Fig. 82 A. E. *Obverse* :—Recumbent bull on a pedestal, facing the left.

Reverse :—In a rectangular enclosure subdivided in four sections is the Telugu legend (Mangama.)

Fig. 83 A. E. *Obverse* :—Recumbent bull to the left.

Reverse :—Tamil legend பழனி (Palani.)

Fig. 83*a* A. E. *Obverse* :—A dagger.

Reverse :—Single fish surround by the Tamil legend பழனி (Palani.)

Fig. 84 A. E. *Obverse* :—A rectangular diagram in the form of a cross.

Reverse :—Single fish, with legend பழனி (Palani.)

Fig. 85 A. E. *Obverse* :—Horse passant to the right.

Reverse :—Tamil legend பழனி (Palani.)

Fig. 86 A. E. *Obverse* :—Horse passant to the right.

Reverse :—Tamil legend விருபாசி (Virupachi.)

Fig. 87 A. E. *Obverse* :—Tamil legend மதுரை (Madurai.)

Reverse :- Telugu legend.........(Madura.)

LIST OF CHOLA COINS

PLATE V

Fig. 88 A. R. *Obverse*:—In the centre is a seated tiger, facing the right, with two fishes and a lamp in front and a bow and a lamp behind. Above these is an umbrella flanked by chamaras (flywhisks.)

Reverse:—The legend in Devanagari characters in two lines उत्तम चोलः (Uttama Cholah.)

Fig. 89 & 93 A. R. *Obverse*:—Same as No. 88, but with the legend श्रीराजेन्द्रः (Sri Rajendrah) in Devanagari characters.

Reverse:—Same as the obverse.

Fig. 90 & 91 A. E. *Obverse*:—Same as No. 88 but with the legend in two lines in Devanagari characters गङ्गैकोण्ड चोलः (Gangai Konda Cholah.)

Reverse:—Same as the obverse.

Fig. 92 A. E. *Obverse*:—Standing figure as in No. 94 (not figured.)

Reverse:—Seated human figure with the Chola Emblem—a seated tiger—to its left. The state umbrella appears above the seated tiger.

PLATE V

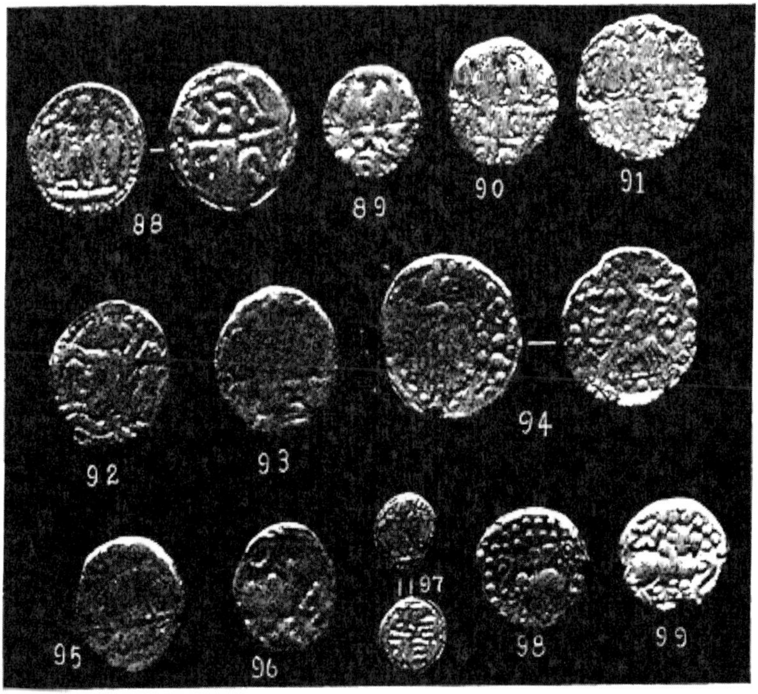

Fig. 94 A. E. *Obverse* :—Standing human figure facing the right, with the lotus flower in its left hand and a trident on its right and other emblems in the field to its left.

Reverse :—Boar standing facing the right with the Canarese legend above (pra......pa.)

Fig. 95 A. E. *Obverse* :—Same as No. 94 (not figured.)

Reverse :—Boar passant to the right.

Fig. 96 A. E. *Obverse* :—Same as No. 94.

Reverse :—Recumbent bull with the couch in front and crescent above.

Fig. 97 A. E. *Obverse* :—A seated tiger (the crest of the Cholas) between two fishes (the crest of the Pandyas) and the bow (the crest of the Cheras) of fig. 88 above.

Reverse :—The legend in Devanagari युद्ध मल्ल (Yuddha malla.)

Fig. 98 A. E. *Obverse* :—Standing figure as in fig. No. 100.

Reverse :—Elephant passant to the left with the Tamil legend, மா (Mara), between the Vaishnava emblems the chank (conch shell) and chakram (discus).

Fig. 99 A. E. *Obverse* :—Standing figure as in figure No. 100.

Reverse :—Standing bull, facing the left with the Canarese syllable "*cho*" above.

Fig. 100 A. E. *Obverse* :—Rudely executed human figure standing for what is fully seen on fig. 108.

Reverse :—Elephant passant to the left with the Tamil legend மா (Mara) with the Vaishnava emblems the chank and chakram (the conch and discus).

Fig. 101 A. E. *Obverse* :—Same as No. 100.

Reverse :—Standing bull facing the right with the Canarese syllable 'vi' in front.

Fig. 102 A. E. *Obverse* :—Same as No. 100.

Reverse :—Standing bull facing the right with the crescent moon above the Canarese syllable 'vi' in front.

Fig. 105 A. E. *Obverse* :—Is the obverse of coins with different reverses as in figures 103, 104, 106 and 107.

Fig. 103 A. E. Recumbent bull with the crescent moon above.

Fig. 104 A. E. Standing bull with the crescent moon above and the "chank" in front.

PLATE VI

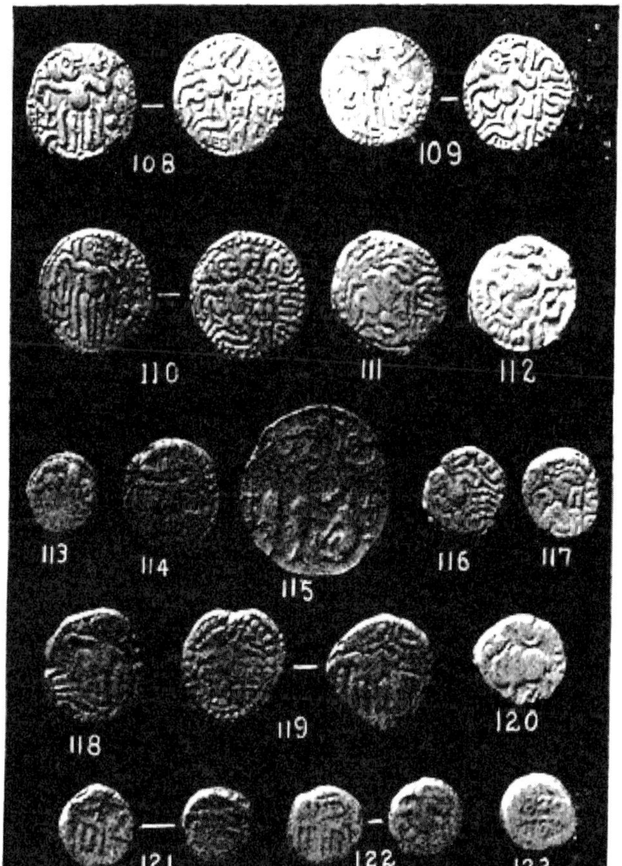

Fig. 106 & 107 A. E. *Obverse*: Standing bull with the crescent moon above and the Devanagari syllable वी (Vi.)

PLATE VI.

Fig. 108 Au. *Obverse*:—Standing figure of the king in regal robes, with the lotus flower in the right hand, the trident in the left hand.

Reverse:—Seated figure of the king with legend श्री लङ्केश्वर (Sri Lankeswara) in Devanagari characters.

Fig. 109 Au. *Obverse*:—Same as No. 108.

Reverse:—Same as fig. No. 108 but with the legend श्री राज राज (Sri Raja Raja) in Devanagari characters.

Fig. 110 Ar, Ae. *Obverse*:—Same as No. 108.

Reverse:—Same as No. 108.

Fig. 111 A. E. *Obverse*:—Same as No. 108 (not figured)

Reverse:—Same as No. 108 but with the legend 'Sri Rajêndra'.

Fig. 112 A. E. *Obverse*:—Same as No. 108.

Reverse:—The seated figure as in 108 with the Tamil legend "ந்த" (nda), probably standing for Sundara.

Fig. 113 A. E. *Obverse*:—Same as No. 100 (not figured).

Reverse:—A galloping horseman.

Fig. 114 A. E. *Obverse*:—Same as No. 100 (not figured).

Reverse:—Seated figure as in No. 108 with the legend in Tamil வி (Vi.)

Fig. 115 *Obverse*:—The seated tiger and two fishes in the field with two three-armed lamps flanking the figures.

Reverse:—The reverse is plain. This figure is the copy of a wax impression of an iron Chola seal.

Fig. 116 A. E. *Obverse*:—Standing figure as in fig. 100 (not figured.)

Reverse:—Seated figure with legend 'रा ஜ., the first syllable in Devanagari and the second in Tamil.

Fig. 117 A. E. *Obverse*:—Standing figure as in No. 100.

Reverse:—Seated figure with legend राज (a small coin, one half of the copper cash usually met with.)

Fig. 118 A. E. *Obverse*:—Standing figure as No. 110.

Reverse:—Seated figure as in No. 110 but with a fish instead of the legend to the left of the figure.

Fig. 119 A. E. *Obverse*:—Standing figure as in No. 110 b. with the "Vishnupādam," to its left.

Reverse :—Seated figure with the legend राज (Raja) as in fig. 110.

Fig. 120 A. E. *Obverse* :—Standing figure as in No. 110.

Reverse :—Bull standing facing the right with the crescent above.

Fig. 121 A. E. *Obverse* :—Standing figure of a flute player with the Tamil syllable வி. (*Vi*) to its left.

Reverse :—Seated figure with the Devanagari legend राज राज (Raja Raja.)

Fig. 122 A. E. *Obverse* :—Same No. 121 but with syllable ரா. (Rä) to the left of the figure.

Reverse :—Same as No. 121.

Fig. 123 A. E. *Obverse* :—Seated figure as in figure No. 121, with legend : Raja-Raja in Devanagari characters.

Reverse :—The Tamil legend in two lines :

சோழன்.

கேசரன்.

Some Inedited Coins of the Kings of Vijayanagara

BY

T. M. RANGACHARI, B.A.

AND

T. DESIKACHARI, B.A., B.L.

It is an admitted fact that **the chronology and succession of many of the princes of the last great Hindu kingdom of the South** are still enveloped in obscurity, in spite of the numerous efforts that have been made in recent times to add to the existing stock of information relating to their history; and the value of coins in clearing up this obscurity will be gathered from a perusal of **Dr. Hultzsch's "Coins of the Kings of Vijayanagara,"** The Indian Antiquary, Vol. XX, p. 301 ff. The list given in that article was an attempt to bring together and present in one view all the available information relating to the coins of the princes of this kingdom, as will be evident from the number of the cabinets that were examined, and the numismatic publications that were consulted, during its compilation. Subsequently, in a further note on South Indian Coins (The Indian Antiquary, Vol. XXI, p. 321 ff.), some Vijayanagara Coins that had not been referred to in the previous list were described. As, however, the coinage of some of the Vijayanagara kings embraced a period of many years, and as some of them had apparently a fancy for issuing coins of various types, the articles above referred to were necessarily not exhaustive, and served only as landmarks for coin collectors, to enable them to distinguish between coins that had already been edited from those that have still to be presented before the numismatic public.

On comparing Dr. Hultzsch's lists with the coins in our cabinet, classified by us as belonging to this series, we discovered that many copper coins in our possession had not been referred to by the learned doctor, and we have accordingly ventured **to supplement his lists by the following notice of some of the inedited coins in our cabinet.** Only such, however, of our inedited coins, as to the readings of the legends on which there was no doubt or uncertainty, have been taken up now, the rest being reserved for examination and notice at a future time.

FIRST DYNASTY

Dêva Râya

Fig. 1—

Obv.—Standing bull, facing the left; the Sun and Moon above; the whole encircled by a ring of dots.

Rev.—The *chank* or conch shell with a sceptre to its left; above the sceptre partly visible the Kanarese letter ದೆ *the*.

The Kanarese letter stands for, or is part of, the full legend **Deva Raya.**

Fig. 2

Obv.—Standing bull, facing the left with a dagger in front; the Sun and Moon above; the whole surrounded by a lined circle.

Rev.—Nagari legend—

श्री	**Sri**
उत्तम	**Uttama**
राय	**Raya**

distributed in three uneven lines amidst other emblems that cannot be deciphered.

Fig. 3—

Obv.—The *chank* and *chakram* (the conch shell and the discus), the usual symbols of Vaishnava worship, separated by a dagger; above the dagger the Moon and below the Sun; the whole surrounded by a lined circle and ring of dots.

Rev.—Nâgarî legend, same as No. 2, with however, the legend distributed around a dagger, the whole surrounded by a lined circle and ring of dots.

Fig. 4.—

Obv.—An elephant passant, to the left; a dagger in front thereof; the Sun and Moon above; the whole within a lined circle and ring of dots.

Rev.—The Nâgarî legend **Uttama Râya,** as in figs. 2 and 3, in three lines, but without any emblems; lined circle and ring of dots as in the last.

We have, with some hesitation, assigned Nos. 2, 3 and 4 to Dêva Râya. They bear a strong resemblance to the coins of the First Dynasty, because it is on these latter, almost exclusively, that the elephant, the bull, the conch, and the discus figure. Of the princes of the First Dynasty the most famous was Dêva Râya, whose reign extended through nearly half a century, and who had issued coins of very various types, chiefly in copper. Though, no doubt, none of the inscriptions, that have been brought to light, allude to Uttama (which means 'best,' and is one of the thousand names of Vishnu) as one of the titles of Dêva Râya, still it is not improbable that this prince had the name of Vishnu put up on his coins, as he is known to have done that of Siva, *viz.*, Nilakantha (blue-necked), on a coin figured as No. 23 in Dr. Hultzsch's list. Further there is nothing incongruous in the same prince adopting the titles of the presiding deities of two rival sects. The policy inaugurated by his father's learned minister Madhava, *viz.*, that of composing the differences between the adherents of rival religious creeds, and in effect reviving the old simple Vedic theology, was in all probability pursued by Dêva Râya, and this must account for the otherwise inexplicable fact, that the coins of his reign bear emblems and figures possessing both Saiva and Vaishnava attributes (as for instance the bull sacred to Siva, and the conch and the discus the emblems of Vaishnava faith).

SECOND DYNASTY

Krishna Râya

Fig. 5—

Obv.—A bull recumbent, facing the left.

Rev.—Nâgarî legend in three lines—

श्री	**Sri**
कृष्णा (रा)	**Krishna (ra)**
(या)	**(ya)**

The middle line alone appears on the coin in full, the rest appearing only in part, as if the coin was too small for the die.

Sadasiva Râya

Fig. 6—

Obv.—Lion passant, to the left.

Rev.—Nâgarî legend in three lines—

(श्री) स	**(Sri) Sa**
दा शि (व)	**da Si(va)**
(राय)	**(Raya)**

Achyuta Râya

Fig. 7—

Obv.—A double-headed eagle holding elephants in its beaks and claws.

Rev.—Nâgarî legend in three lines—

श्री (प्र)	**Sri (pra)**
(ता) पाच्यु (त)	**(tâ) pachyu (ta)**
(राय)	**(Raya)**

This is the copper prototype of the gold pagoda, fig. 29, Dr. Hultzsch's first list.

Fig. 8—

Obv.—Prancing horse, to the left.

Rev.—Nâgarî legend in three lines—

श्री (प्र)	**Sri (pra)**
(ता) पाच्यु (त)	**(tâ) pachyu (ta)**
(राय)	**(Raya)**

THIRD DYNASTY

Venkapati Râya

Fig. 9—

Obv.—The figure of Hanuman, or the Monkey-God, advancing to the right.

Rev.—Nâgarî legend in three lines—

श्रीवें	**Sri Ven**
कपति	**kapati**
राय	**Raya**

Our thanks are due to Dr. E. Hultzsch, Government Epigraphist, Bangalore, at whose instance the plaster casts, from which the accompanying plate was copied, were prepared by M. R. Ry. B. Santappa Garu, Curator of the Mysore Government at Bangalore.

INDO-DANISH COINS

T. M. RANGACHARI AND T. DESIKACHARI.

No authentic information exists regarding the history of the **Danish Mint at Tranquebar,** but as far as can be gathered, the Danes in India struck there no fewer than three hundred varieties of coins in lead, copper, silver and gold. It does not appear that there was any mint in the other Danish Settlements in India, *viz.*, at Porto Novo, Serampore, or Balasore.

Out of the three hundred varieties above mentioned only about eighty can now be obtained in India. Many of these were published by us in 1888,[1] and the rest have been recently dealt with by Dr. E. Hultzsch, Government Epigraphist, Bangalore.[2] One remarkable piece, however, has hitherto remained unpublished, and that is **the lead Cas of Frederick III.** (A. D. 1648-70) :—

Obv.—The crowned monogram of the king—F. 3.

Rev.—The Royal escutcheon of Denmark.

By far the oldest and the most difficult to obtain of the **Tranquebar issues** are those **in lead** ; and when met with, they are so much oxidised, that it is scarcely possible to decipher the legend on them. Lead was coined into money only in the first three reigns, and the coinage commenced with Christian IV, in the year

---

[1] "Indo-Danish Coins": *Madras Journal Literature and Science* for the Session 1888-89.

[2] *Indian Antiquary*, Vol. XXII, pp. 116-122.

1640; but the earliest lead coin bearing date, so far as we know, was of the year 1644. None of these lead issues bear on them the value of the coin, in this particular differing from the later copper coinage. The coins of Christian IV, indeed, have on them the legend *Cas*, but even then, the exact value is omitted. Unlike the copper issues also, the lead ones were of numerous varieties, not less than a dozen different kinds of coins being stated to have been struck in the reign of Frederick III alone. Some of them afford a clue to the place of mintage, Tranquebar, by the presence on them of the letters D. B. or T. B., standing for Dansborg (the Fort at Tranquebar) or Tranquebar; and in the reign of Christian V it appears to have been usual to insert on the coins the initials of the mint officer: thus, W. H. [van] K. [alnien].

It would be both a useful and an interesting enquiry to ascertain how it was that a metal so easily liable to decay as lead, came to be chosen as a medium of currency during the infancy of the Indo-Danish Settlement. That in early days there was a scarcity of this metal is evident from the records of the travellers who then visited India. The author of the *Periplus* mentions tin and lead among the imports of Baragaza[1] (Bharôch) on the Western Coast, and of Nelkunda[2] (conjectured by Col. Yule to have been between Kanetti and Kolum in Travancore). Sir Walter Elliott also refers to a passage in Pliny, where it is stated that "India has neither brass nor lead receiving them in exchange for precious stones and

[1] *The Commerce and Navigation of the Erythræan Sea,* by J. W. McCrindle, M.A., (Trübner and Co., 1879) p. 122.

[2] *Ibid.* p. 136.

pearls."[1] The only ancient Hindu kingdom that is known to have possessed a lead currency was that of the Andhras, and Sir W. Elliott has suggested that the scarcity of lead in those days might afford some explanation for this peculiarity in the Andhra coinage.[2]

Coming to later times, we meet with a lead currency only with the advent of the several European powers in the East. The Indo-Portuguese are known to have coined lead money; and the English East India Company, in imitation of the Portuguese, obtained of Charles II a charter authorizing them to coin, among others, 'budgrooks' (Port *bazarucco*),[3] lead coins, which appear to have been issued by the English East India Company in the reign of Charles II and in those of the first three Georges, for currency in the Settlement at Bombay.[4] Whether the scarcity of lead, felt in the early centuries of the Christian era, continued up to so late a period as the 16th and 17th centuries, is not known; but it is not improbable that lead was still popular as a medium of currency, and it was perhaps to suit this taste of their customers that the earliest European Power in India, the Portuguese, struck lead coins. The English and the Indo-Danish Companies appear to have copied the Indo-Portuguese in this respect.

It is not known why this currency was subsequently abandoned, but it is remarkable that all the European powers began to give it up just about the same time.

---

[1] *Numismata Orientalia—Coins of Southern India*, p. 22. [2] *Op. cit., loc. ci*

[3] *History of the Coinage of the East India Company* (Government Press Madras), by Edgor Thurston, Esq., pp. 16 and 17.

[4] *Ibid.* pp. 19, 25, 26 and 33.

Copper coins appear to have been issued from the Indo-Danish Mint for the first time in the reign of Frederick III, the earliest copper coin bearing date being of the year 1667 A. D.

The late Lieut-General Pearse sent us a drawing of a large **tutenag** coin which he believed to have been issued in the reign of Christian IV (1588-1648):—

Obv.—The crowned cipher of the king.

T. R.
Rev.—C. A. S.
1644.

But we have not hitherto met with this, or any other *tutenag* coins from the Danish Mint.

As in the lead, so in the copper, coinage of Tranquebar, the exact value was not designated on the coins in the reigns of Frederick III and Christian V, and the first attempt made at giving this was in the reign of Frederick IV (1699-1730), who issued 10, 4 and 2 *KAS* pieces. This system continued till 1845, the date of the final cessation of the Danish Power in India.

None of the published lists, however, refer to, nor have we been able to obtain, X. *KAS* pieces of the reigns of Frederick V (1746-1766), or of Christian VI (1730-1746). But during the long reign of Christian VII two types of X. *KAS* were issued. The earlier variety had on its obverse the double linked monogram of the king and on its reverse the monogram of the *Dansk Asiatisk Compagni* with the date and value. The later variety had on its obverse the single crowned monogram and on the reverse the value and the date.

Likewise there were two varieties of IV. *KAS*, both bearing on their obverse the monogram C7. On the reverse of the earlier variety were figured the monogram of the Company and the date and the value, but on that of the later variety the date and value alone appeared without the monogram. When this change took place, and whether it pointed to a total release of all their claims by the Danish Company in the East Indian Danish Settlements in favor of the Crown, are matters as to which it is not possible to obtain any exact information.

From 1808 to 1814, the Fort and Town of Tranquebar were, owing to hostilities between the mother countries, taken possession of and retained by the Madras Army. During this period no coins at all were issued, the Danes having naturally suspended operations Tranquebar was restored to the Danish Power in 1814.

Silver coins began to be struck in the reign of Christian V (1670-1699), and the earliest known coins are the five and two *fanos* of 1683. The silver currency thus started in *fanos*, conformably to the then popular monetary system of India, was superseded in 1755, by the introduction of the one and two *royaliner*. The change was, however, only nominal, the value of the *royalin* continuing to be nearly equal to one-eighth of a rupee. In 1816 a return was made to the old nomenclature *fanos*, which continued till 1818, from which year, the Danish Mint ceased to coin silver.

So far as we know, there were no Indo-Danish gold *fanams*, and the only gold coin that appears to have been struck was the pagoda of Christian VII:—

Obv.—The crowned monogram of the king ℭ on a granulated surface.

Rev.—An Indian idol.

From the description given of it in the accompanying list of the Copenhagen Collection, it appears that the pagoda of Christian VII must have resembled in appearance and size the earlier variety of the Star Pagoda (*Pulivarâhan*) of the English East Indian Company.

Another gold coin is mentioned in the Copenhagen Royal Coin Cabinet *Catalogue*:—

Obv.—The crowned monogram of the king ℭ.

Rev.—ح the Persian initial, of Haidar, so familiar to collectors of Mysore coins of the Muhammadan Usurpation period.

This coin is of very great interest, as tending to shew that the Danish power in the East did homage to the Mysore Usurper, consistently with the unambitious policy of peace adopted by them in their dealings with the dominant Indian Powers.

We now append a **list of the Indo-Danish coins in the Royal Coin Cabinet, Denmark,** probably the largest known collection of these coins. The list was furnished in March 1884, by Mr. C. F. Herbert, Inspector of the Royal Coin Cabinet at Copenhagen, to the late Lieut.-General Pearse, who kindly placed at our disposal his notes on Indo-Danish coins, including the list. Both have been of material help in the preparation of this paper.

Coins of the Danish Colony in East India (Tranquebar).

(B. signifies the work *Beskrivelse over danske Mynter og Medailler i den Kgl Samling* (Kjöbenhavn

1791, in folio, in which many of the coins are engraved.)

Christian IV, 1588-1648.

Lead

1. *Obv.*—The king's crowned cipher C4.

Rev.—T. R. CAS, 1644 (Tranquebar cash).

2. *Obv.*—As No. 1.

Rev.—Cas.

3. *Obv.*—As No. 1.

Rev.—IHS (*B. Tab.* XXV No. 32).

Frederick III, 1648-1670

Copper

1. *Obv.*—The king's crowned cipher: beneath CAS, 1667.

Rev.—The Norse Lion.

2. Similar, but without year and of smaller size (*B. Tab.* XXI 13).

Lead

All with the same obverse: crowned F. 3.

3. *Rev.*—A lion and nine hearts (arms of Cimbria).

4. *Rev.*—A swan and S. (arms of Stormorn).

5. *Rev.*—A Lamb of God (arms of Gothia).

6. *Rev.*—A nettle (arms of Holstein).

7. *Rev.*—A crowned stock-fish and A (arms of Iceland).

8. *Rev.*—A rose.

9. *Rev.*—A cross: +.

10. *Rev.*—A cross and the letters I. C.: I†C

11. *Rev.*—D. B. (perhaps Dansborg) and an indistinct indication of the year.

Christian V, 1670-1699

Copper

1. *Obv.*—The king's cipher set two-fold under a crown, between 8—9 (1689).

   Rev.—Crowned D. O. C. between W.—H. and beneath v. K. (*B. Tab.* XXV No. 1b,

1b. Similar, from the year 1691.

2. *Obv.*—The king's crowned double cipher.

   1 D. O. C. 6
   Rev.—Crowned 92 (*B. Tab.* XXI No. 19).

3, 4. Similar, from the years 1694 and 1697 (*B. Tab.* XXXV 11, No. 15 and XLI No. 3).

Lead

5. *Obv.*—Crowned 16 C5 87.

   Rev.—Crowned D. O. C. / W. K.

6. *Obv.*—Crowned 8 C5 9.

   Rev.—Crowned W. D. O. C. H. K.

7. *Obv.* Crowned C5.

   Rev.—Crowned D. O. C.

8. *Obv.*—C5.

   Rev.—DC.

Frederick IV, 1699-1730

Silver

1. Double Fano.

   Obv.—Crowned 17 F4 31.

Rev.—The Norse Lion.

This coin was struck before the king's death $\frac{12}{10}$ 1730 was known in India.

2. Fano ($\frac{1}{8}$ Rupee).

Obv.—Crowned 17 F4 30.

Rev.—The Norse Lion (*B. Tab.* XXIX No. 7).

Copper

3. *Obv.*—The king's crowned double cipher.

DOC

Rev.—Crowned 10

Kass.

4. *Obv.*—As No. 3.

Rev.—DOC
4 Kas.

5. *Obv.*—As No. 3.

Rev.—DOC
2 Kas.

6. (Kas).

Obv.—As No. 3.

Rev.—Crowned DOC.

7. (Kas).

Obv.—Crowned F4.

Rev.—Crowned DOC. (*B. Tab.* XXIX No. 17-19).

Christian VI, 1730-1746

Silver

1. Double Fano.

Obv.—Crowned 17 C6 31.

Rev.—The Norse Lion (*B. Tab.* XIII No. 3.)

2. Fano, of similar type and same year.

Copper

3. 4 Kas.

Obv.—Crowned C6.

Rev.—Crowned DAC (Dansk Asiatisk Compagnie).
4

(*B. Tab.* XIV No. 10.)

4. 2 Kas. Similar type but DAC (*B. Tab.* XIV
2
No. 11).

5. (Kas). Similar type but DAC (*B. Tab.* XIV No. 12.)

6. (Kas).

Obv.—Crowned 17 C6 31.

Rev.—The Norse Lion.

7. (Kas). Similar from the year 1732.

8. (Kas).

Obv.—C6.

Rev.—DAC.

9. (Kas).

Obv.—C6.

Rev.—TB (= Tranquebar).

Frederick V, 1746-1766

Silver

1. 2 Royaliner (= Fanos).

Obv.—Crowned F5.

Rev.—The value and beneath, the crowned Danish escutcheon between 17-55 (*B. Tab.* XIX No. 23).

2-7. Similar, 1756, 1762, 1764 (*B. Tab.* XIX No. 24). 1765-1766 and *sine anno.*

Copper

16. 4 Kas.

Obv.—Crowned ℱ.

Rev.—Crowned 17 DC 61 (*B. Tab.* XIX No. 18).
4

17. 4 Kas. Similar from the year 1763 (*B. Tab.* XIX No. 18).

18. Kas.

Obv.—As No. 16.

Rev.—Crowned 17 DC 61.

Christian VII, 1766-1808

Gold

1. Pagoda.

Obv.—Crowned C7.

Rev.—Indian idol (weight 1 ducat).

2. Pagoda.

Obv.—Crowned C7.

Rev.— ح, the Persian H (Haidar 'Ali).

This coin is not known in the Danish Collections. The description is taken from *Neueste Münzkunde Abbildung und Beschreibung der jetzt coursirenden Gold und silbermünzen.* 1ster Band (Liepzig 1853) Taf. LIX No. 1.

Silver

3. 2 Royaliner.

Obv.—Crowned C7.

Rev.—The value over the Danish escutcheon between 17—67.

4-28. Similar from 1768, 1770, '71. '72, '73, '74, '75, (*B. Tab.* XIII 5), 1776, '79, '80, '81, '83, '84, '86 (variant 17—$\frac{86}{R}$), '87, '88, '89, '92, '94, '95, '96, '97, '99 and 1807.

29. Royalin. Similar type as No. 3 from the year 1767.

30-55. Similar from 1768, '69, '70 (*B. Tab.* XIII 3), 1771, '73, '74, '75, '76, '79, '80, '81, '83, '84, '86, 17—$\frac{86}{R}$, '87, '88, '89, '91, '92, '93, '94, '95, '96, '97, '99 and 1807.

Copper

56. 10 Kas.

Obv.—Crowned C7.

DC

Rev.—10 KAS

A° 1768

57-58. Similar from 1770 and 1777 (*B. Tab.* XIII 9).

59. 10 Kas.

Obv.—As. No. 56.

X

Rev.—Kas

1786

60-61. Similar from 1788-1790.

62. 4 Kas.

Obv.—Crowned C7.

Rev.—Crowned 17 $\frac{DC}{4}$ 67.

63-65. Similar from 1768, 1770 (*B. Tab.* XII No. 11) and 1777.

66. 4 Kas.

Obv.—Crowned ℭ.

IV
Rev.—Kas
1782

67-75. Similar from 1786, var. 1786/R, 1787, 1788, '89, '90, '97, '99, 1800, 1807.

76. 2 Kas.

Obv.—Crowned ℭ.

Rev.—Crowned 17 DC/S 80 (*B. Tab.* XIII 15).

77. Similar with 17 DC/2 70.

78-79. Kas.

Obv.—Crowned ℭ.

Rev.—Crowned 17 DC/1 77; and similar from 1780 (*B. Tab.* XIII 16).

Frederick VI, 1808-1839

Silver

1. 2 Fano.

Obv.—Crowned F VI.

* 2 *
Rev.—FANO
1816

2. Similar from 1818.

3-4. Fano. Similar type as No. 1, but the value 1/FANO from 1816 and 1818.

Copper

5. 10 Kas.

Obv.—As No. 1.

* X *
Rev.— KAS
1816

6-8. Similar from 1822, 1838 and 1839.

9. 4 Kas.

Obv.—As No. 1.

* IV *
Rev.— Kas
1815

10-24. Similar from 1816, '17, '20, '22, '23, '24, '25, '30, '31, '32, '33, '34, '37, '38 and 39.

25. Kas.

Obv.—As No. 1.

1
Rev.—KAS
1819

Christian VIII, 1839-1848

Copper

1. 10 Kas.

Obv.—Crowned

* X *
Rev.— KAS
1842

2. 4 Kas.

Obv.—As No. 1.

* IV *
Rev.— KAS
1840

3. Similar from 1841, '42, '43, '44 and '45.